S I M P L Y

SIMPLY GOURMET, EVERY DAY

D1064782

SIMPLY.

SIMPLY GOURMET, EVERY DAY

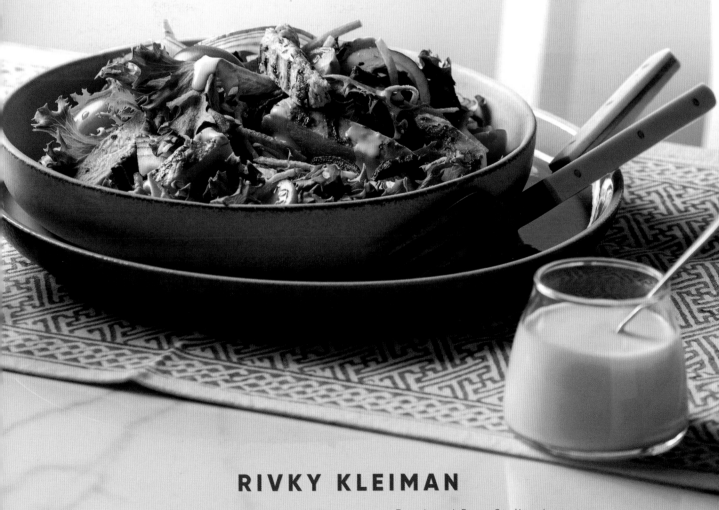

RIVKY KLEIMAN

Photography by
CHAY BERGER

Food and Prop Styling by
RENEE MULLER

© Copyright 2021 by **Mesorah Publications, Ltd.**
First Edition — First Impression / November 2021

ALL RIGHTS RESERVED

No part of this book may be reproduced in any form, photocopy, electronic media, or otherwise — even for personal, study group, or classroom use — without written permission from the copyright holder, except by a reviewer who wishes to quote brief passages in connection with a review written for inclusion in magazines or newspapers.

THE RIGHTS OF THE COPYRIGHT HOLDER WILL BE STRICTLY ENFORCED.

Published by ARTSCROLL / SHAAR PRESS
313 Regina Avenue / Rahway, NJ 07065 / (718) 921-9000 / www.artscroll.com

Distributed in Israel by SIFRIATI / A. GITLER
POB 2351 / Bnei Brak 51122 / Israel / 03-579-8187

Distributed in Europe by LEHMANNS
Unit E, Viking Business Park, Rolling Mill Road Jarrow, Tyne and Wear, NE32 3DP / England

Distributed in Australia and New Zealand by GOLDS WORLD OF JUDAICA
3-13 William Street / Balaclava, Melbourne 3183 / Victoria, Australia

Distributed in South Africa by KOLLEL BOOKSHOP
Northfield Centre / 17 Northfield Avenue / Glenhazel 2192 / Johannesburg, South Africa

ISBN-10: 1-4226-2991-0 / ISBN-13: 978-1-4226-2991-8

Printed in the United States of America

ACKNOWLEDGMENTS

I thank *HaKadosh Baruch Hu* for the inspiration, the ability, and the gift to be able to come to this day. I take nothing for granted. I am grateful for all He has given me and with which He continues to bless me.

To my husband: Any gratitude that I express needs to be multiplied many times over. Thank you, BB, for your support, for your guidance, and most of all, for completing me.

Huda, Zisi, Yechiel, Shana, Hadassah, Shlomo, Yaakov, Hindy, Sari, Ari, and Shimi: Thank you for making me the luckiest mother/grandmother. I truly appreciate your support throughout this entire project. It would not have been possible without you!

Ema (my bouncer off-er) and Abba: You set the bar really high. I thank you for being my greatest champions and encouraging me to follow my dreams. I love you and aspire to be like you.

To my family and extended family: Thank you for encouraging and believing in me and, best of all, for being the most awesome "FAM."

To my *"MISHPACHA,"* with my friend and editor *Chanie Nayman* at the helm: Thank you for being friends and family and an awesome support system.

Rabbi Gedaliah Zlotowitz: You are a true visionary and leader of the most amazing ArtScroll team. May Hashem continue to bless you *ad meah v'esrim*. It is truly a pleasure to work with you.

To my editor, the fabulous *Felice Eisner:* Second time around ... practically perfect in every way.

Judi Dick, Jenna Grunfeld, and Shana Halpert: Your keen eyes will assure a well "proofed" read.

Devorah Cohen: Your creativity and passion to get it just right are so appreciated. Thank you for putting everything you've got into this project to ensure that each page in this book is 100%.

Renee Muller, food stylist par excellence: Your dedication to assure that each picture is as perfect as possible is legendary. You are professional and cutting edge. Above all, you are a friend.

Chay Berger: Thank you for bringing all my recipes to life with your magnificent photography and impeccable eye.

Miriam (Pascal) Cohen and Leah Schapira: I appreciate your cheering me on and helping this cookbook be even better.

Thank you to my "KitchenAids," *Nechama Beren, Mashie (Shirken) Dickisson, Hindy Kleiman, Shana Kleiman, Tzippy Levine, Sari Rubnitz, and Hadassah Weinberg:* For keeping me company in the kitchen on those long days of photo-shooting.

Hindy Kleiman and Esther Leah Sandhaus: Thank you for once again helping put my thoughts and words onto paper. I could not have completed this project without you!

Colorush Marketing (www.colorush.com): You did it again. Thank you for this magnificent cover and layout design. Your talent never ceases to amaze me.

Special thanks to: *The Fishing Line of Lakewood:* One taste and you'll be "hooked," and *Epstein's Meat of Lakewood, NJ:* Your meat is always a "cut above."

Special appreciation to *Sari Rubnitz:* Your creativity is appreciated both in the kitchen and on social media.

Meesh Pasternak and Chaim Goldgrab: Your attention to detail is legendary. Thank you for sharing your talents.

Nechama Beren: Family by chance — friend by choice; thank you for always being there for me.

Last but not least, those who have just been there for me: *Chaya Suri Leitner, Sina Mizrahi, Naomi Nachman, Danielle Renov, Rorie Weisberg, and Moshe Wulliger.*

3

TABLE OF CONTENTS

Contents

SIDES

DESSERTS

BAKED GOODS

SIMPLE SUPPER

Special shout-out to my amazing recipe-testing team. I appreciate you taking the time to follow each recipe to a T and giving me honest feedback to assure that each recipe is simply perfect!

Tova Beer • Chay Berger • Nechama Beren • Devorah Cohen • Miriam (Pascal) Cohen
Huvie Eisenreich • Felice Eisner • Chanie Follman • Chanie Gelman • Raizel Halon
Hindy Kleiman • Judy Kleiman • Shana Kleiman • Zisi Kleiman • Batsheva Leibowitz
Renee Muller • Chani Pechter • Esti Rubnitz • Sari Rubnitz • Baila Sandhaus
Esther Leah Sandhaus • Chani Schlisselfeld • Simi Silberberg • Yitzy Taber • Yael Taub
Hadassah Weinberg • Daniella Zlotowitz

AUTHOR'S PREFACE

TO MY READERS,

After **Simply Gourmet** was released, the requests kept coming in, at a demo, via Instagram and email, or in the supermarket: We LOVE your cookbook! We need more, we need simple, we need tips and tricks on how to cook gourmet, without a huge investment of time. I appreciate all of your feedback and your many requests. I heard you loud and clear! That inspired me to bring you more: to help achieve *Simply Gourmet Every Day*.

My nephew, Chaim, throughout the COVID lockdown, called me every day for clarification when he was helping his mother with suppers. Over the many months, he became quite a seasoned chef. Recently, he called to say, "Tante Rivky, I'm an expert already on this whole cookbook — when is the next one coming out?"

This book was designed to make your life just a little bit easier, to provide you with recipes that are simply gourmet — *simple to create, gourmet on your plate — EVERY DAY!* From weekdays to Shabbos, from parties to *simchas* — there is something for everyone — for every occasion.

This cookbook will give you more focus on cooking **SIMPLY** with incredible taste and quality. In your busy life there is no need to give up your desire to cook, bake, and serve delicious food, as long as it's done **SIMPLY** and with ingredients you will generally have on hand.

Thank you for once again allowing me into your kitchens.

Happy cooking,

Rivky R

SIMPLE SUPPER

It is not usually recommended to skip to the end of a book ...
but in this case it is highly recommended.

Life has become so fast-paced that one aspect of my goal is to alleviate
the stress of feeding families in record time. Turn to page 302 and you
will see just how easy dinner can be. Each simple supper includes:

| MENU PLANNING AND PAIRING | • | PREP AHEAD | • | TOTAL PREPARATION AND COOKING TIME | • | TIPS AND TRICKS |

In addition, you will find some recipes throughout the book
that include a "simple supper" icon in the far left corner of the page.
These recipes meet very strict criteria:

1. **Prep time must be no longer than 10 minutes total.**

2. **The food must be ready to serve in less than an hour.**

Some "simple supper" recipes that fit these guidelines can have dinner on the table
within 30 minutes!

To easily identify the level of difficulty of each dish,
look for the number and type of utensils pictured:

A spoon means that
the recipe is simple and
beginner level.

A spoon and a knife
indicate a recipe requiring
intermediate skill and
somewhat more prep time.

A spoon, knife, and fork
signify a lengthy process
or a more advanced level
of expertise.

In My Kitchen ...

My preferences when it comes to basic ingredients are as follows:

BLACK PEPPER

I use coarsely ground black pepper.

BROWN SUGAR

When a recipe calls for brown sugar, it refers to dark brown sugar unless otherwise specified.

CRUSHED GARLIC

Nothing compares to fresh garlic, crushed. I always use a garlic press, which allows me to put the clove in unpeeled. The press allows the crushed garlic through and leaves the peel behind. Just clean the press between each clove; it takes only a moment and eliminates the need for peeling.

LEMON JUICE

Fresh is always preferable.

MILK

I use 1%.

NONDAIRY MILK

All are terrific choices. I particularly enjoy oat, cashew, and macadamia milk.

OLIVE OIL

I always use the extra light olive oil.

SALT

My two favorites are **sea salt** and **kosher salt**. I use Diamond Crystal brand kosher salt flakes. If you use Morton's, reduce each teaspoon by ¼, as the crystals are more concentrated. For sea salt, I use fine grain. For the ultimate garnish or crunch, I use **Maldon flaky salt**.

VANILLA

When a recipe calls for vanilla, it refers to pure vanilla extract. The recipe will specify if vanilla sugar is called for. Vanilla is a flavoring in which quality makes a tremendous difference. My preference is always pure vanilla extract.

BAKING SHEETS

I use only metal sheet pans, as they conduct heat evenly and retain the heat better, resulting in a more complete roast on veggies. Disposable pans will need longer roasting time and it may not yield an even roast.

Before You Begin ...

After you decide to prepare a recipe, it's very important that you read the recipe from start to finish before beginning to cook. Then you can be sure that you have all the ingredients and utensils needed.

Starters

CUBED FIRECRACKER SALMON

Pareve   YIELDS *8 servings*

Inspired by the ever-popular fire poppers sauce, I decided to give it a try and expand on the craze. Nestled on a bed of angel hair pasta, these nuggets are truly fabulous.

1½-2 lb skinless salmon fillet, cut into 1-inch cubes

Firecracker Sauce

2-4 Tbsp sriracha, as per your heat preference

¼ cup dark brown sugar

¼ cup honey

3 Tbsp low sodium soy sauce

3 cloves garlic, crushed

½ tsp sea salt

Angel Hair Pasta Salad

16 oz angel hair pasta, prepared according to package directions

½ cup sesame oil

½ cup low sodium soy sauce

¼ cup balsamic vinegar

1 Tbsp hot chili flavored oil *or* **2½ tsp** olive oil + **1-1½ tsp** hot sauce

¼ cup sugar

1 tsp black sesame seeds + additional for garnish

• scallions *or* chives, for garnish

1. Preheat oven to 400°F. Line a baking sheet with parchment paper.

2. Combine firecracker sauce ingredients in a resealable bag or bowl. Reserve a few tablespoons of sauce for basting post-baking. Add salmon cubes to sauce; toss to coat. Marinate for 30 minutes.

3. **Meanwhile, prepare the angel hair pasta salad:** In a large bowl, combine sesame oil, soy sauce, balsamic vinegar, chili oil, sugar, and 1 teaspoon sesame seeds. Add prepared angel hair pasta to the dressing. Toss well to combine. Set aside.

4. Place salmon cubes on prepared baking sheet. Bake for 12 minutes. Baste with reserved sauce.

5. **To assemble:** Place a small mound of angel hair pasta in the center of each plate. Nestle 3 salmon cubes over pasta. Garnish with a light sprinkling of sesame seeds and scallions. Serve at room temperature.

TUNA TARTARE TOWER

Pareve YIELDS *6 servings*

Need a dramatic meal opener? With this modern presentation of a classic dish, your guests are sure to be wowed.

Tuna Tartare

1½ lb	sushi grade tuna, finely diced
2 Tbsp	lime juice
1 Tbsp	low sodium soy sauce
1 Tbsp	sesame oil
2 tsp	rice vinegar
½ -1 tsp	ground ginger *or* **1 cube** frozen ginger
1 tsp	kosher salt
¼ tsp	coarsely ground black pepper
1 clove	garlic, crushed *or* **1 cube** frozen garlic

Sweet Sauce

½ cup	low sodium soy sauce
½ cup	sugar
½ cup	mirin

Guacamole

2-3	avocados, diced
2 Tbsp	lime juice
1 Tbsp	avocado oil
½ tsp	kosher salt
½ tsp	garlic powder

Optional Garnishes

1	jalapeño pepper, seeded and finely diced
1 small	red onion, finely diced
•	black sesame seeds
2 Tbsp	panko crumbs
•	fresh parsley *or* chives
•	spicy mayo

1. **Prepare the sweet sauce:** Combine sauce ingredients in a small saucepan. Bring to a boil over medium-high heat.

2. Reduce heat; gently simmer until thickened and reduced by half, 15-17 minutes. Do not over boil or sauce will not be pourable consistency.

3. Remove from heat and cool. Sauce will thicken more as it cools. Transfer to a squeeze bottle or container. Store in the refrigerator until ready to use.

4. **Prepare the tartare:** Place tuna into a medium bowl. Add remaining tartare ingredients; stir to combine. Set aside for 10 minutes for flavors to meld.

5. **Prepare the guacamole:** Place diced avocados into a small bowl. Add remaining guacamole ingredients. Stir or mash according to your preference.

6. **Traditional serving suggestion:** Spray a ramekin with nonstick cooking spray or line with plastic wrap. Fill three-quarters full with tuna mixture, pressing down with a spoon. Sprinkle with 1 tablespoon panko crumbs. Top with guacamole. Place serving plate over ramekin; invert to release. Drizzle with sweet sauce or serve sauce in a small bowl on the side; garnish with toppings of choice.

7. **Modern serving suggestion (pictured):** Spray 2 different-sized ramekins with nonstick cooking spray or line with plastic wrap. Fill one with tuna mixture and one with guacamole. Place serving plate over ramekins; invert to release. Alternatively, this can be done by filling ring molds on serving plate and then removing the molds. Drizzle with sweet sauce or serve sauce in a small bowl on the side; garnish with toppings of choice.

— Tip

To get neat slices, cut tuna while it is partially frozen.

BAKED KANI BITES

Pareve YIELDS *28 bites*

I had accidentally defrosted a package of kani and wanted to come up with a different way to prepare it than my usual go-to. These bites, together with their dipping sauce, are a welcome new addition to my repertoire.

¼ cup	mayonnaise
1	egg
4	scallions, white and light green parts only, finely diced
2 Tbsp	lemon juice
1 Tbsp	whole grain mustard
1 tsp	Worcestershire sauce
1 tsp	Old Bay seasoning
1 sleeve	snackers crackers, crushed
•	sea salt, to taste
•	coarsely ground black pepper, to taste
3 Tbsp	nondairy milk
10 oz	kani, finely diced
¼ cup	fresh parsley leaves, chopped, *or* 2 Tbsp dried parsley flakes
•	lemon wedges, optional
•	lettuce leaves, for garnish, optional

Lemon-Mustard Dipping Sauce

¾ cup	mayonnaise
¼ cup	oil
¼ cup	fresh parsley leaves, chopped, *or* 2 Tbsp dried parsley flakes
2 Tbsp	lemon juice
1 Tbsp	whole grain mustard
1 tsp	honey
1	dill pickle, finely diced
1 tsp	hot sauce
•	sea salt, to taste
•	coarsely ground black pepper, to taste

1. **Prepare the lemon-mustard dipping sauce:** In a small bowl, combine all dipping sauce ingredients. Mix well. Refrigerate until ready to serve.

2. Preheat oven to 375°F. Line a baking sheet with parchment paper.

3. **Prepare the kani bites:** In a medium bowl, stir together mayonnaise, egg, scallions, lemon juice, mustard, Worcestershire sauce, and Old Bay seasoning. Stir in crushed crackers, salt, pepper, and nondairy milk. Fold in kani and chopped parsley until well combined. If time allows, chill for 20-30 minutes.

4. Using a tablespoon or small scoop, shape mixture into 28 (1½-inch) balls. Place on prepared baking sheet.

5. Bake 20 minutes, until lightly browned. Serve bites with dipping sauce and lemon wedges and/or lettuce leaves, if using. May be served warm or at room temperature.

CRUNCHY CAULIFLOWER POPPERS

Pareve or Dairy

YIELDS *6 servings*

2	eggs, lightly beaten
½ cup	fine panko crumbs
½ cup	matzah ball mix
½ tsp	onion powder
½ tsp	garlic powder
½ tsp	sea salt
24 oz	fresh or frozen cauliflower (see Note)

Sweet Chili Dipping Sauce

½ cup	mayonnaise
¼ cup	sweet chili sauce
½ tsp	paprika

Dairy Ranch Dipping Sauce

3 Tbsp	mayonnaise
3 Tbsp	sour cream
3 Tbsp	milk
1 Tbsp	dried parsley flakes
2 tsp	vinegar
¼ tsp	garlic powder
⅛ tsp	sea salt
⅛ tsp	onion powder
pinch	black pepper

Being mindful of healthy eating, I set out to devise an alternative to frying without compromising on the crunch factor. When you dunk these oven-baked crispy goodies into either of these fabulous dips, I know you'll agree that healthier options can be just as delicious.

1. Preheat oven to 400°F. Line a baking sheet with parchment paper; coat with cooking spray.

2. In a small bowl, lightly beat eggs. In another small bowl, combine panko, matzah ball mix, and seasonings.

3. Dip each cauliflower floret into egg mixture; roll in crumb mixture until completely coated. Place coated florets in a single layer on prepared baking sheet. Spray florets generously with cooking spray.

4. Bake 20 minutes on center rack.

5. **Prepare dipping sauces:** In a small bowl, whisk together sweet chili dipping sauce ingredients. For dairy meals, in a second bowl, also whisk together dairy ranch dipping sauce ingredients (see Variation).

6. Serve warm or at room temperature.

Note

If using frozen cauliflower, run under hot water to defrost; drain well before coating.

Variation

Dairy Ranch Dipping Sauce can be made pareve by using nondairy sour cream and nondairy milk.

PASTRAMI-WRAPPED PORTOBELLO MUSHROOMS

Meat YIELDS *18 stacks*

At a Sheva Berachos for my dear friend and fellow cookbook author Miriam (Pascal) Cohen, I presented this dish. In moments the whole serving tray was polished off and had to be replenished. Best way to let me know what a winner this dish is.

12 oz	sliced portobello mushrooms
¼ cup	low sodium soy sauce
¼ cup	honey
2 Tbsp	mirin
2 cloves	garlic, crushed
1 tsp	toasted sesame oil
12 oz	sliced pastrami

1. In a large resealable bag, combine soy sauce, honey, mirin, garlic, and sesame oil. Mix well. Add mushrooms. Seal; turn bag to ensure all mushrooms are coated. Marinate for 30 minutes.

2. Stack 2 mushroom slices. Wrap ½ slice pastrami around stack. Use a toothpick to pierce through the pastrami and mushrooms and secure the pastrami slice. Repeat with remaining mushrooms and pastrami. Brush pastrami with marinade.

3. Preheat oven to 400°F. Line a baking sheet with parchment paper.

4. Transfer mushroom stacks to prepared baking sheet. Bake on center rack for 25-28 minutes. Delicious served warm or at room temperature.

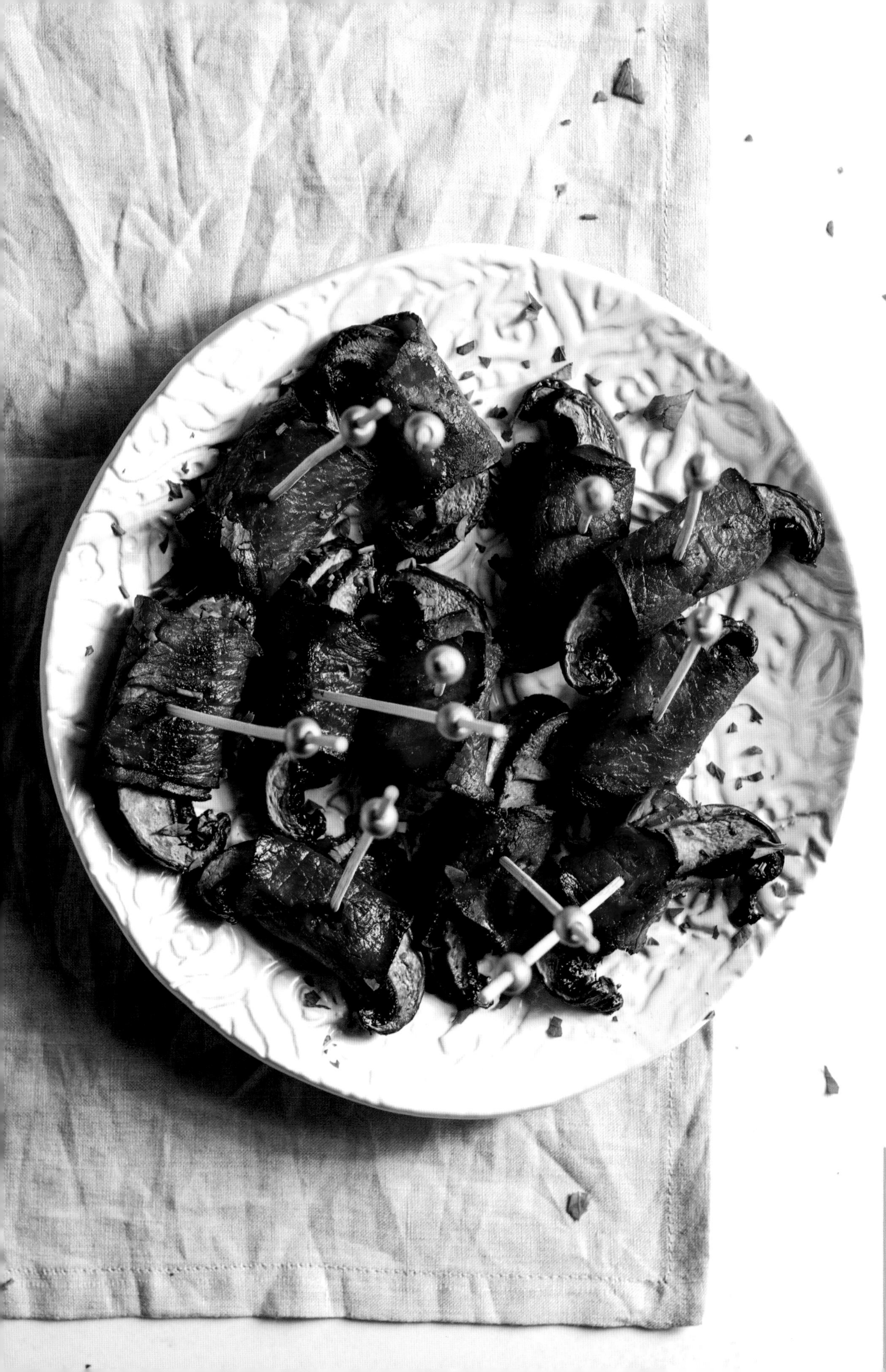

BEEF JERKY DUO

This perfect finger food is a great anytime snack. In my home, there are lots of beef jerky lovers. It was always the first of the Shabbos treats to vanish. My kids challenged me to make my own and offered to be the official taste testers. After some trial and error, my kids finally proclaimed it "the best jerky around."

Meat   YIELDS *10 servings*

2 lb London broil

Chili Lime Marinade

⅓ cup	low sodium soy sauce
¼ cup	lime juice, preferably fresh
2 Tbsp	fish-free Worcestershire sauce
2 Tbsp	sweet chili sauce
2 Tbsp	honey
2 Tbsp	chili lime rub
1 Tbsp	dark brown sugar
1 tsp	liquid smoke

Teriyaki Marinade

¾ cup	low sodium soy sauce
½ cup	teriyaki sauce
¼ cup	fish-free Worcestershire sauce
2 Tbsp	brown sugar
1 Tbsp	honey
2 tsp	onion powder
1½ tsp	liquid smoke
1½ tsp	smoked paprika
1½ tsp	pure maple syrup
1 tsp	garlic powder
1 tsp	coarsely ground black pepper
½ tsp	sea salt
½ tsp	crushed red pepper flakes

1. If time allows, to ease slicing, place meat into the freezer for 1 hour. Thinly slice across the grain into ¼-inch-thick slices.

2. Combine preferred marinade ingredients in a large resealable bag. Add sliced meat to the bag. Mix until completely coated. Marinate in the fridge overnight.

3. Remove meat from marinade. Discard remaining marinade.

4. **To use a dehydrator:** Place meat in a single layer on dehydrator racks. Set dehydrator to 160°F. Run dehydrator for 2 hours. Lower dehydrator temperature to 145°F. Run for an additional hour, for a total of 3 hours.

5. **To use an oven:** Preheat oven to 185°F. Place wire racks over 2 baking sheets. Place meat in a single layer on racks. Bake for 3 hours, turning slices after 90 minutes.

6. Remove meat from racks; cool. Store in an airtight container for 1 week or refrigerate for longer shelf life.

Tip

Many ovens have a dehydrator feature, so use that feature to keep the dehydrator pareve.

CLASSIC CHILI

Meat YIELDS *6-8 servings*

This is a classic chili recipe, only better! It is made in minutes and can be a welcome change for a weeknight dinner as well.

1 Tbsp	olive oil
1 large	onion, diced
3 cloves	garlic, crushed
1 lb	ground beef
2½ Tbsp	chili powder
2 Tbsp	sugar
1 Tbsp	kosher salt
½ tsp	coarsely ground black pepper
½ tsp	hot sauce
1½ cups	beef broth *or* **1½ cups** water + **1½ tsp** beef broth powder
1 (15-oz) can	fire-roasted diced tomatoes
1 (15-oz) can	red kidney beans, drained and rinsed
1 (8-oz) can	tomato sauce
½ cup	tomato juice
1 Tbsp	lime juice

1. In a large skillet, over medium-high heat, heat olive oil. Add onion and garlic; sauté for 5 minutes, stirring occasionally. Add ground meat. Break apart beef clumps with a wooden spoon. Cook for 6-7 minutes until brown, stirring mixture occasionally.

2. Add chili powder, sugar, salt, pepper, and hot sauce. Stir until combined. Add broth, diced tomatoes with their juice, beans, tomato sauce, tomato juice, and lime juice.

3. Bring chili to a boil. Reduce heat to medium. Simmer, uncovered, for 20-25 minutes, stirring occasionally.

4. Remove from heat. Serve warm.

CRISPY CHICKEN FINGERS

Meat   YIELDS *8 servings*

Easy to prepare oven-baked crispy goodness.

2 lb	chicken cutlets, cut into wide strips
½ cup	nondairy milk
2 Tbsp	low sodium soy sauce
1 Tbsp	yellow mustard
1 tsp	hot sauce
2	eggs
4 cups	crisp rice cereal, crushed
2 tsp	onion soup mix
2 tsp	garlic powder
2 tsp	paprika
1 cup	flour

Sweet and Sour Dipping Sauce

½ cup	water, divided
¼ cup	vinegar
¼ cup	ketchup
2 Tbsp	dark brown sugar
2 Tbsp	sugar
1 Tbsp	lemon juice
1 tsp	hot sauce
1½ Tbsp	cornstarch

1. Preheat oven to 400°F. Line 2 baking sheets with parchment paper; coat with cooking spray.

2. In a medium bowl, whisk together nondairy milk, soy sauce, mustard, hot sauce, and eggs.

3. In a second bowl, combine crushed cereal with onion soup mix, garlic powder, and paprika.

4. Place flour on a plate.

5. Dredge chicken in flour, then in egg mixture, and finally very well in seasoned cereal. Place chicken on prepared baking sheets. Coat with cooking spray.

6. Bake, uncovered, for 25 minutes.

7. **Meanwhile, prepare the sweet and sour dipping sauce:** In a small saucepan over medium heat, combine 6 tablespoons water, vinegar, ketchup, sugars, lemon juice, and hot sauce. Bring to a boil. In a small cup, combine remaining 2 tablespoons water with cornstarch to form a slurry; add to sauce. Stir continuously over medium heat until mixture is well combined and thickened.

8. Serve chicken with dipping sauce.

LAMB TORPEDOES

Meat   YIELDS *16 torpedoes*

With their herby vibe and mouthwatering aiolis, you won't be able to stop eating these. Be sure to double the aioli sauces. They are so good that you'll want to use them on everything.

2 lb	ground lamb
1	egg
¼ cup	grated onion
3 cloves	garlic, crushed
1 tsp	dried parsley flakes
1 tsp	sumac, optional
¾-1 tsp	dried oregano
1 tsp	kosher salt
½ tsp	coarsely ground black pepper
pinch	cayenne pepper
3 Tbsp	extra light olive oil

Creamy Lemon-Garlic Aioli

½ cup	mayonnaise
2 cloves	garlic, crushed
2 Tbsp	lemon juice
4 tsp	olive oil
1 tsp	lemon zest

Horseradish Aioli

½ cup	mayonnaise
2 Tbsp	prepared white horseradish
1 Tbsp	lemon juice
½ tsp	smoked paprika

Special Equipment

16	wooden skewers, soaked in water for 20-30 minutes

1. Preheat oven to 400°F. Line a baking sheet with parchment paper.

2. In a large bowl, combine lamb, egg, onion, garlic, parsley, sumac (if using), oregano, salt, pepper, and cayenne. Form mixture into 16 torpedoes; thread onto soaked skewers. Place on prepared baking sheet.

3. Brush torpedoes with oil; bake until golden and cooked through, about 20 minutes, turning torpedoes after 10 minutes.

4. Alternatively, grill torpedoes. Heat grill; grill torpedoes for 3 minutes. Flip; grill for an additional 3-5 minutes.

5. **Prepare the aiolis:** In a small bowl, whisk together all creamy lemon-garlic aioli ingredients. In a second bowl, whisk together all horseradish aioli ingredients.

6. Serve torpedoes warm or at room temperature, accompanied by the aioli dipping sauces.

— Variation —

Any ground meat can be subbed in for the lamb.

SANGRIA

Pareve

YIELDS *8 (5-oz) servings*

1 (750-ml) bottle	Morad Lychee wine, chilled
½ **cup**	frozen lemonade concentrate, thawed and strained
½ **cup**	orange juice, strained
½ **cup**	cranberry juice cocktail, chilled
½ **cup**	cold seltzer, chilled
1	orange
1	lemon
1 cup	frozen cranberries
8	cinnamon sticks

Festive, fruity, and fun, sangria is great for entertaining a group of adults and it's easy to customize with your favorite wine and fruit. To release their flavors and essential oils, twist the orange and lemon strips before adding to the cups.

1. **Prepare the garnishes:** Peel orange and lemon neatly with a knife to form strips of peel; set aside. Cut orange and lemon into half-moons; set aside.

2. Pour wine, lemonade concentrate, orange juice, cranberry juice, and seltzer into a pitcher. Mix to combine. Divide evenly between 8 cups.

3. Garnish each cup with orange and lemon slices and peels, cranberries, and a cinnamon stick.

Notes

For a sweeter sangria, use ginger ale in place of seltzer.

Lychee wine can be substituted with any sparkling white or fruity wine of choice.

Tip

Straining the lemonade concentrate and orange juice through a fine mesh sieve helps achieve a clear drink, if preferred.

Variation

Blend wine mixture with ice to make an alcoholic slushie.

RASPBERRY LEMONADE

Pareve   YIELDS *6 servings*

1¼ cups freshly squeezed
         lemon juice

5 cups   water

• ice cubes

Raspberry Syrup

1½ cups water

¾ cup   sugar

1½ cups frozen raspberries

Raspberries give this sweet, tart, and refreshing lemonade its fruity flavor and vibrant pink color. It's aesthetically appealing with a taste to match, so ever since my first sip, I always keep a pitcher on hand.

1. **Prepare the raspberry syrup:** Combine sugar and water in a medium pan over medium heat. Stir until all the sugar has dissolved. Stir in raspberries; bring to a boil. Reduce heat; simmer until raspberries break down, 3-4 minutes.

2. Strain raspberry syrup through a cheesecloth or fine sieve. Allow to cool.

3. **Prepare the raspberry lemonade:** In a large pitcher, whisk together lemon juice, water, and raspberry syrup. Refrigerate until chilled. Serve over ice.

Variation

Add ½-1 cup vodka for a great adult drink!

Dairy Delights

SUMMER SQUASH PLATTER

Dairy   YIELDS *4 servings*

Broil this simple summer or year-round side in your oven. In just a few minutes, this perfectly tender squash is ready to enjoy. Charred and seasoned sublimely, this beautiful platter is a real crowd-pleaser.

2   zucchini, not peeled

2   yellow squash,
          not peeled

¼ cup chopped sundried
          tomatoes

½ cup crumbled feta cheese

Marinade/Dressing

⅓ cup   olive oil

2 Tbsp   lemon juice

2 cloves garlic, crushed

½ tsp   sea salt

¼ tsp   coarsely ground
             black pepper

1. Wash and dry zucchini and squash. Slice diagonally into ½-inch rounds.

2. **Prepare the marinade:** In a small bowl, combine marinade ingredients. Pour half the marinade into a large resealable bag. Set aside the remaining marinade to be used as the dressing.

3. **Prepare the squash:** Add zucchini and squash slices to the bag; toss to coat. Marinate for 1 hour or overnight in the fridge.

4. Preheat oven to broil. Line a baking sheet with parchment paper.

5. Remove zucchini and squash slices from marinade; place on prepared baking sheet. Broil for 3 minutes. Flip slices; broil for an additional 3 minutes. Alternatively, grill slices on each side. Set aside to cool.

6. Add chopped sundried tomatoes to reserved marinade. Whisk together to combine.

7. Arrange zucchini and squash slices on a platter. Drizzle with sundried tomato dressing. Top with crumbled feta cheese. Serve at room temperature.

THREE-CHEESE STUFFED MUSHROOMS

Dairy

YIELDS *12 stuffed mushrooms*

Packed with seasoned cheesy goodness, these are a party-perfect or anytime treat.

12 medium	mushroom caps
⅓ **cup**	cottage cheese
⅓ **cup**	crumbled feta cheese
⅓ **cup**	sour cream
1 tsp	garlic salt
1 tsp	dried chives *or* parsley + more for garnish
⅓ **cup**	shredded mozzarella cheese

1. Preheat oven to 350°F. Set out a 9x13-inch baking pan.

2. Remove mushroom stems; remove gills. Clean caps by wiping with a moist paper towel. Place mushrooms into prepared pan.

3. In a bowl, combine cottage cheese, feta cheese, and sour cream. Season with garlic salt and chives. Stir until well combined. Fill each mushroom cap with cheese mixture. Top with shredded mozzarella cheese.

4. Cover pan with foil. Bake for 20 minutes. Uncover; bake an additional 10 minutes. Serve warm. Garnish with additional chives or parsley.

TWICE-BAKED EGGPLANT BOATS

Dairy   YIELDS *2-4 servings*

Cheesy and easy, these stuffed eggplant boats are a great alternative to pasta. If you've never been a fan of eggplant, this simple and satisfying vegetarian dish is sure to change your mind.

1 medium	eggplant
2 Tbsp	olive oil
pinch	kosher salt
pinch	black pepper
1 Tbsp	butter
1	onion, diced
3 cloves	garlic, crushed
1 cup	shredded cheddar cheese
½ cup	grated Parmesan cheese
1	egg, beaten
2 tsp	dried basil
½ tsp	dried oregano
½ tsp	sea salt
¼ tsp	coarsely ground black pepper

1. Preheat oven to 375°F. Set out a baking pan or oven-to-table cookware large enough to hold eggplant halves securely.

2. Wash and dry eggplant. Cut in half lengthwise. Using a sharp paring knife, cut a 1-inch dice pattern into the flesh of the eggplant, being careful to cut down ¼-inch but not through the skin of the eggplant. Place, cut-side up, into prepared pan. Drizzle with olive oil and a pinch of salt and pepper. Bake, uncovered, for 25 minutes. Remove from oven. Lower oven temperature to 350°F.

3. When eggplant is cool enough to handle, scoop out eggplant flesh, leaving ¼-inch shell. Return eggplant halves to pan; set aside. Cut eggplant flesh into cubes; set aside.

4. In a skillet, over medium-high heat, melt butter. Add onion and garlic; sauté for 5 minutes. Add cubed eggplant; sauté for an additional 5 minutes.

5. In a medium mixing bowl, combine cheeses, egg, basil, oregano, salt, and pepper. Add eggplant mixture. Stir well to combine. Divide mixture between eggplant shells.

6. Bake eggplant, uncovered, for 40 minutes. Turn oven to high broil. Broil for 3-5 minutes, until lightly golden. Serve warm.

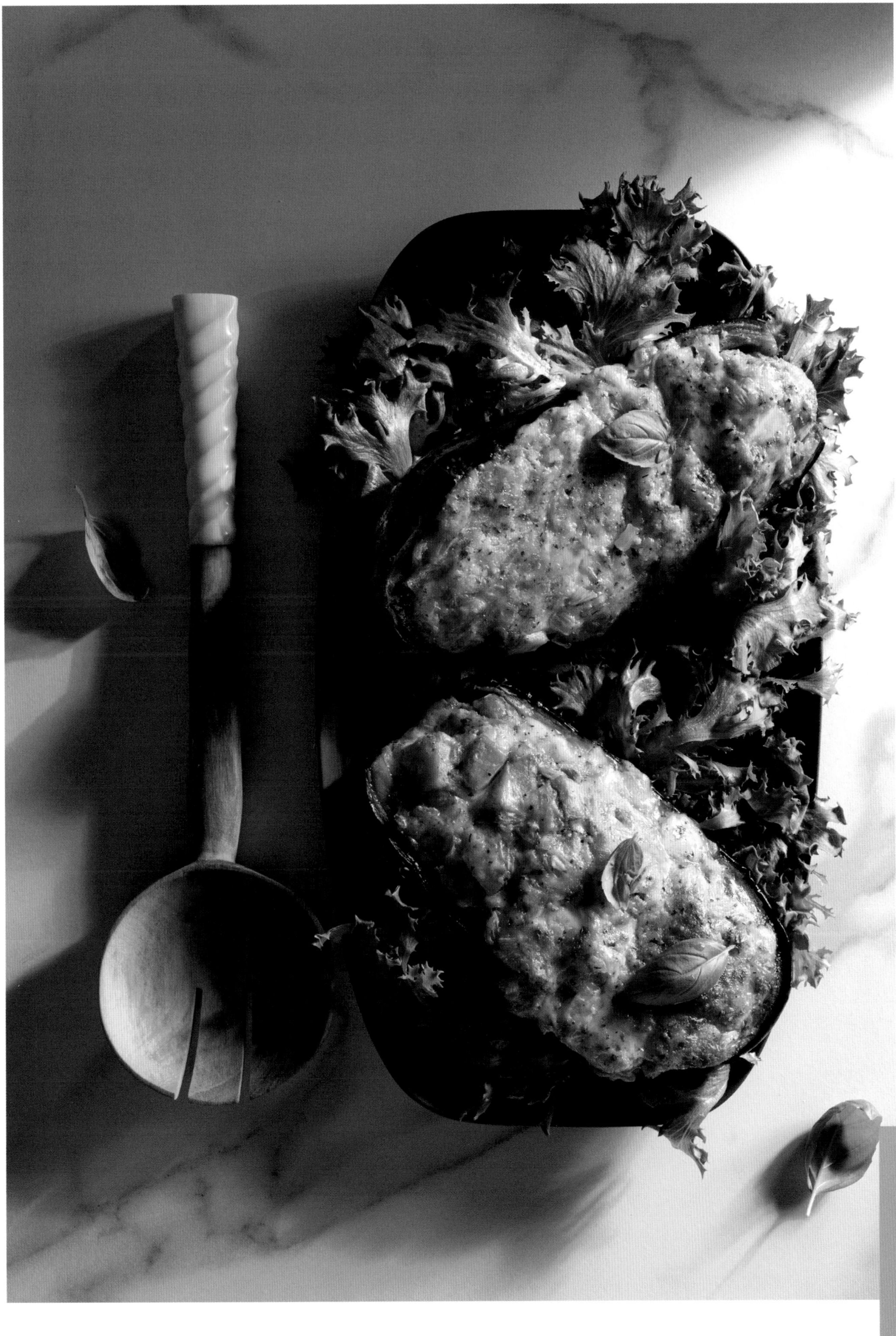

CHEDDAR CHEESE TART

Dairy YIELDS *6 servings*

2 Tbsp	butter
1 large	onion, diced
8 oz	cheddar cheese, grated
3	eggs
1 cup	heavy cream
½ tsp	sea salt
¼ tsp	coarsely ground black pepper
¼ tsp	ground mustard

While dreaming up a new quiche concept, I thought that a cheese base would be a welcome change. This light, crustless gem is quick and easy to throw together in a pinch.

1. Preheat oven to 375°F. Coat a 9-inch round oven-to-table baking dish or pan with cooking spray; set aside.

2. In a medium skillet, over medium heat, melt butter. Add onion; sauté until golden, about 8 minutes.

3. Add grated cheese to prepared baking dish, evenly coating the bottom. Spread sautéed onion over cheese.

4. In a medium bowl, combine eggs, heavy cream, salt, pepper, and ground mustard. Mix well. Pour over onions.

5. Bake for 45 minutes. Rest for 15-20 minutes before cutting.

─ Note ──────────────

You may substitute Swiss or pepper jack for the cheddar.

HOMEMADE MARINARA SAUCE

Pareve   YIELDS *11 cups*

2 Tbsp	olive oil
1 large	onion, diced
4 large cloves	garlic, crushed
2 (15-oz) cans	tomato sauce
2 (6-oz) cans	tomato paste
2 (15-oz) cans	crushed tomatoes
2 (15-oz) cans	stewed tomatoes with their liquid
1 tsp	kosher salt
1 tsp	dried basil
1 tsp	dried oregano
½ tsp	dried rosemary
½ tsp	dried thyme
½ tsp	coarsely ground black pepper
4	bay leaves

Its rich and lively tomato flavor tastes immeasurably better than store bought. Once you start making this, you'll never buy jarred marinara sauce again. Thanks, Tanta Chumi, this one is definitely a keeper.

1. In an 8-quart pot over medium-high heat, heat olive oil; add onion and garlic. Sauté for 5 minutes, until softened. Add all remaining sauce ingredients. Bring mixture to a boil. Reduce heat; simmer for 1 hour, stirring occasionally. Remove and discard bay leaves.

2. For a smooth marinara sauce, purée with an immersion blender. For a chunky marinara sauce, leave it as is.

— Tip

This marinara sauce is freezer friendly. Divide, freeze, and use as needed.

STUFFED SHELLS

Dairy   YIELDS *30 shells*

When I introduced this dish to my family, I knew it was a hit. The creamy texture and cheesy goodness in the shells coupled with the flavorful homemade marinara turned a normally chatty bunch into a silent group, focused on finishing their first helping to ensure their seconds, before it was all gone.

4 cups	homemade marinara sauce *or* store-bought marinara
1 (12-oz) package	jumbo pasta shells
1 (16-oz) container	cottage cheese
1 (8-oz) container	whipped cream cheese with garlic *or* plain whipped cream cheese mixed with **2 cloves** crushed garlic
½ cup	sour cream
3½ oz	grated Parmesan cheese *or* white cheddar cheese
1	egg
½ tsp	kosher salt
½ tsp	coarsely ground black pepper
½ cup	chopped fresh chives

1. Preheat oven to 350°F. Coat a 9x13-inch baking dish with cooking spray.

2. Bring a large pot of salted water to a boil. Add pasta; cook for 3 minutes less than the recommended cooking time for al dente. Drain pasta; rinse under cold running water.

3. In a large bowl, combine cottage cheese, cream cheese, sour cream, grated cheese, egg, salt, pepper, and chives.

4. Pour marinara sauce into the dish and spread to cover the entire bottom of the dish.

5. Spoon cheese mixture into shells. Nestle shells into the marinara sauce.

6. Bake, covered, for 25 minutes.

-Tip

The stuffed shells are freezer friendly.

FRESH SPINACH FETTUCCINE

Dairy   YIELDS *2-4 servings*

Surprisingly easy with simply gourmet results. You'll be amazed how feta cheese becomes a creamy pasta sauce and takes this dish to the next level.

¼ cup	butter
1 large	shallot, finely minced
½ cup	dry white wine
1 cup	heavy cream
1 cup	feta cheese, crumbled, divided
2 Tbsp	chopped fresh parsley leaves *or* **¾ Tbsp** dried parsley flakes
8-10 oz	fresh spinach fettuccine *or* pasta of choice, prepared according to package directions

1. In a large skillet, over medium-high heat, melt butter. Add shallot; sauté for 2 minutes. Add wine; simmer until liquid has reduced by half. Stir in heavy cream; simmer until sauce thickens slightly, 2-3 minutes. Add ½ cup feta cheese and parsley. Stir to combine.

2. Place cooked pasta into a serving dish. Pour sauce over pasta; toss to combine. Sprinkle with remaining ½ cup feta cheese.

PENNE WITH ROASTED VEGETABLES

Dairy YIELDS *4-6 servings*

Whether you choose to omit the cheese and simply serve the pasta and veggies as a salad (see Variation) or prepare it as directed and serve it as a meal, this dish is an all-around winner and really hits the spot.

3 Tbsp	lemon juice, preferably fresh
3 Tbsp	red wine vinegar
2 cloves	garlic, crushed
3 tsp	dried basil or **3 cubes** frozen basil
1½ tsp	dried parsley flakes *or* **1 cube** frozen parsley
¼ tsp	crushed red pepper flakes
1½ tsp	kosher salt, divided
½ tsp	coarsely ground black pepper, divided
½ cup	olive oil + more for brushing
2	colored peppers, quartered
1	red onion, sliced into thick rings
1	zucchini, cut into thick planks
16 oz	penne *or* pasta of choice, prepared according to package directions
1 cup	shredded mozzarella *or* muenster cheese

1. In a small bowl, whisk or blend together lemon juice, vinegar, garlic, basil, parsley, and red pepper flakes. Add ½ teaspoon salt and ¼ teaspoon black pepper. Slowly add 9 tablespoons olive oil by hand, whisking until combined. If using a blender, set it on low speed while slowly adding olive oil until combined. Set dressing aside.

2. Preheat oven to high broil. Line a baking sheet with parchment paper.

3. Place vegetables on prepared baking sheet. Brush vegetables with olive oil. Sprinkle with remaining salt and pepper. Broil 5-8 minutes. Allow to cool; dice all vegetables.

4. Set oven temperature to 350°F. Set out a 9x13-inch baking pan.

5. Place cooked pasta into prepared pan. Add diced vegetables, dressing, and shredded cheese. Toss to coat.

6. Bake for 15 minutes, or until cheese has melted. Remove from oven, stir, and serve immediately.

Variation

This dish can be made pareve by omitting the cheese. Place cooked pasta into a serving bowl. Add broiled vegetables and dressing. Toss to coat. Serve immediately.

Note

This dish will stay fresh in the refrigerator for 4 days.

RAVIOLI WITH MUSHROOM VODKA SAUCE

Dairy   YIELDS *6-8 servings*

As a penne a lá vodka fan and mushroom lover, pairing these two was a dream come true. The mushrooms, garlic, and creamy vodka sauce deliver fabulous flavor and a rich, delicious meal.

3 Tbsp	olive oil
1 small	onion, diced
4 cloves	garlic, crushed
2 Tbsp	chopped flat parsley leaves *or* **1 tsp** dried parsley flakes
12 oz	white mushrooms, thinly sliced
8 oz	shiitake mushrooms, stems removed, thinly sliced
•	kosher salt, to taste
2 Tbsp	butter
2 cups	heavy cream
26 oz	vodka sauce *or* marinara sauce
¾ cup	grated Parmesan cheese
¼-½ tsp	coarsely ground black pepper
2 (10-12-oz) packages	cheese ravioli, fresh or frozen, prepared according to package directions

1. In a large skillet, over medium-high heat, heat oil. Add onion; sauté until translucent. Add garlic; continue to sauté until mixture turns golden.

2. Add parsley, stir. Add mushrooms. Season mixture with generous pinch of salt. Cover; lower heat to medium. Cook for 10-15 minutes. Uncover; continue to cook until all liquid is absorbed.

3. Add butter, stirring until melted and combined. Add heavy cream. Raise heat to high. Cook 3-4 minutes, stirring occasionally, to reduce cream until it thickens. Reserve 2 tablespoons grated cheese for garnish. Add vodka sauce, remaining grated cheese, and black pepper. Mix to combine. Taste; adjust seasonings if needed.

4. Add prepared ravioli to the sauce. Toss and serve. Garnish with reserved grated cheese.

LEMON-TARRAGON QUINOA BOWL

Dairy YIELDS *2-3 servings*

Quinoa bowls are a great and easy way to turn what you have in the fridge into a healthy, filling meal This roasted veggie quinoa bowl has three tasty components and only requires fifteen minutes of your time.

1 cup	raw quinoa, prepared according to package directions (see Note)
8 oz	button mushrooms *or* baby bella mushrooms
1 small	eggplant, diced
1 small	red onion, sliced
1 small	onion, sliced
1	red pepper, sliced
1 cup	shredded or spiralized carrots
3 Tbsp	olive oil
1 Tbsp	kosher salt
1 tsp	coarsely ground black pepper
½ cup	crumbled feta cheese

Lemon-Tarragon Dressing

•	zest of 1 lemon
2 Tbsp	lemon juice, preferably fresh
2 Tbsp	Dijon mustard
1 tsp	dried tarragon
1 tsp	honey
½ tsp	kosher salt
¼ tsp	coarsely ground black pepper
½ cup	canola oil

1. Preheat oven to low broil. Set out a baking sheet.

2. Place vegetables on prepared baking sheet. Drizzle with olive oil, salt, and pepper. Broil for 7-10 minutes. Remove from oven; set aside to cool.

3. **Prepare the lemon-tarragon dressing:** Whisk together dressing ingredients until combined and emulsified.

4. **To assemble:** Place prepared quinoa into each bowl. Top with roasted vegetables, sprinkle with feta, and drizzle with dressing.

—Note—

For added flavor when preparing quinoa, add 1 packet ranch dressing mix or 2 tablespoons broth powder of choice to the water.

ONION BOARD WITH HERBED BUTTER

Dairy YIELDS *8-10 servings*

Similar to focaccia, this fluffy bread is topped with the sweet taste of caramelized onions. Perfect with your eggs and favorite soup, and a great way to feed your hungry troops after a long fast.

Dough

2¼ tsp	dry yeast
1½ cups	warm water
¼ cup + 1 Tbsp	sugar, divided
4½-5 cups	flour
1	egg
¼ cup	oil
1 Tbsp	kosher salt

Topping

3 Tbsp	olive oil
2 medium/ large	onions, finely diced
1 tsp	kosher salt
1 tsp	poppy seeds
1	egg, slightly beaten

Herbed Butter

¼ cup	unsalted butter (½ stick), softened
1 Tbsp	dried parsley flakes
1 tsp	garlic powder
½ tsp	kosher salt

1. **Prepare the herbed butter:** In a small bowl, mix ingredients together until well combined. Place into a ramekin and cover, or shape into a log and wrap in plastic wrap. Freeze for 1 hour, until firm; transfer to the refrigerator.

2. **Prepare the dough:** In a large measuring cup, combine yeast, water, and 1 tablespoon sugar. Proof mixture for 5-7 minutes.

3. Place flour, remaining ¼ cup sugar, egg, oil, and salt into the large bowl of an electric mixer fitted with the dough hook. Pour proofed yeast over flour mixture. Mix well for about 5 minutes until a sticky dough forms. Alternatively, the mixture can be kneaded by hand. Transfer dough to a greased bowl; set aside to rise for 1 hour.

4. **Prepare the topping:** In a large frying pan, over medium heat, heat oil. Add diced onions; sauté until translucent. Add salt; sauté, stirring occasionally, for 20 minutes, until onions are golden brown. Set aside.

5. Coat a baking sheet with cooking spray; sprinkle liberally with flour. Lightly flour a sheet of parchment paper the size of the baking sheet.

6. Turn dough out onto prepared parchment paper. Roll dough out into a rectangle the size of the parchment paper. Lift paper and turn over to transfer the dough to prepared baking sheet. Remove and discard parchment paper. Press dough into all corners of the baking sheet, stretching if necessary.

7. Brush the entire top of the dough with beaten egg. Spread caramelized onions evenly over the entire dough, then sprinkle with poppy seeds. Let rest for 30 minutes.

8. Preheat oven to 350°F. Bake for 30 minutes. Allow to cool before cutting into squares or sticks. Serve with herbed butter.

RAISIN BRAN BRUFFINS

Dairy YIELDS *16 muffins*

2 cups	raisin bran cereal
1½ cups	milk
½ cup	honey
¼ cup	canola oil
2	eggs
1½ cups	whole wheat flour
1 Tbsp	baking powder
½ tsp	baking soda
½ tsp	sea salt
2 tsp	pure vanilla extract

One of my favorite cereals in a breakfast muffin! These are so moist, hearty, and healthy, with just the right amount of sweetness. Great breakfast on the go for those busy mornings or an anytime fiber-filled snack.

1. Preheat oven to 375°F. Line 16 muffin cups with paper liners or coat with cooking spray.

2. In a medium bowl, combine cereal and milk. Let stand for 5 minutes. Add honey, oil, and eggs. Stir to combine. Add dry ingredients and vanilla, mixing until just combined. Do not over-mix.

3. Spoon batter into prepared muffin cups, two-thirds full.

4. Bake 16-18 minutes, until muffins spring back lightly to the touch.

FRENCH TOAST CHURROS

Dairy YIELDS *12 roll-ups*

The most insanely delicious French toast you will ever have. When my grandson who is really a picky eater gave it two thumbs up, I knew we had a winner. Try it and see for yourself; every bite of these caramel-filled churro roll-ups will leave you wanting more.

12 slices	white bread, crusts removed
6-8 Tbsp	caramel sauce, homemade or store-bought
½ cup	milk
2	eggs
1 Tbsp	sugar
1 tsp	cinnamon
½ tsp	vanilla sugar
pinch	kosher salt
•	pancake syrup, optional
•	whipped cream, optional

Cinnamon Sugar Coating

½ cup	sugar
¼ cup	dark brown sugar, packed
2 tsp	cinnamon

Chocolate Sauce

3½ oz	good quality chocolate, chopped
½ cup	heavy cream
1 Tbsp	butter, melted
2 Tbsp	light corn syrup

1. Preheat oven to 400°F. Line a baking sheet with parchment paper; coat with cooking spray.

2. Using a rolling pin (or a bottle), roll out bread slices as thinly as possible.

3. Place caramel sauce in microwave for 20 seconds to soften. Spread each slice of bread with caramel sauce. Roll up, jelly roll-style, as tightly as possible. Set aside.

4. In a medium bowl, combine milk, eggs, sugar, cinnamon, vanilla sugar, and salt. Whisk until combined.

5. **Prepare the cinnamon sugar coating:** In a small bowl, stir together coating ingredients until combined.

6. Dip each roll-up in the milk mixture to evenly coat; then dip and evenly coat in the cinnamon sugar coating. Place on prepared baking sheet.

7. Bake 13-15 minutes.

8. **Prepare the chocolate sauce:** Place chopped chocolate and butter into a bowl. In a small saucepan, heat heavy cream until bubbles start to form, but do not bring to a boil. Pour heated heavy cream over chopped chocolate and butter. Allow to sit for 5 minutes to melt the chocolate. Add corn syrup; stir to combine.

9. Serve churros with chocolate sauce and/or pancake syrup and whipped cream.

BABI'S BUTTER BUNS

Dairy

YIELDS *approximately 36 buns*

1½ cups	warm water
3 Tbsp	dry yeast
1 cup + 1 Tbsp	sugar, divided
6 cups	flour
1 cup	butter (2 sticks), softened
3	eggs
1 tsp	kosher salt
1 Tbsp	vanilla sugar

Butter Filling

1½ cups	butter (3 sticks)
1 cup	powdered sugar
2 tsp	vanilla sugar

Milk Glaze

1 cup	milk
2 Tbsp	sugar

My friend Yael's Babi is renowned for her butter buns. This recipe originated with her family in Hungary and has continued to be an enduring legend for generations. I am pleased to present my version of Babi's famous butter buns.

1. In a small bowl, combine water, yeast, and 1 tablespoon sugar. Proof for 15 minutes.

2. To the bowl of an electric mixer fitted with the dough hook, add flour, remaining 1 cup sugar, butter, eggs, salt, and vanilla sugar. Create a well. Pour proofed yeast mixture into the well. Beat on low speed until all ingredients are combined. Increase speed to medium; knead for 5 minutes until a beautiful workable dough forms.

3. Grease a large bowl with oil. Place dough into greased bowl. Cover; set aside to rise for 1 hour or until doubled in size.

4. **Prepare the butter filling:** Using an electric mixer, beat together butter and sugars until smooth.

5. Divide dough into 3 pieces. Work with one piece of dough at a time. Line 2 baking sheets with parchment paper.

6. On a lightly floured surface, roll out one piece of dough into a thin rectangle. Smear dough with one-third of the butter filling. Begin to roll, jelly roll-style. Pull dough while rolling to achieve a tight roll. Slice into 1-inch rounds; place on prepared baking sheets. Cover buns; allow to rise for 30 minutes.

7. Repeat with remaining dough and filling.

8. Preheat oven to 350°F.

9. **Prepare the milk glaze:** In a small bowl, combine milk and sugar, stirring to dissolve sugar.

10. Bake buns for 20 minutes. Remove from oven. Drizzle glaze over buns. Return to oven for an additional 5 minutes. Remove from oven; allow to cool.

---Tip---

For optimal flavor, roll out dough thinly and roll buns tightly.

STREUSEL-TOPPED BANANA CARAMEL MUFFINS

Dairy YIELDS *12 muffins*

With pockets of sweet caramel and streusel topping, these are sure to be your new favorite muffin. Even your non-banana lovers will give it two thumbs up.

2	ripe bananas
1 tsp	lemon juice
1¾ cups	flour
½ cup	sugar
½ cup	dark brown sugar
1 tsp	baking powder
½ tsp	baking soda
½ tsp	sea salt
½ cup	canola oil
¼ cup	heavy cream
2	eggs, lightly beaten

Filling

¼ cup	caramel sauce , homemade or store-bought

Streusel Topping

½ cup	flour
¼ cup	dark brown sugar
4 Tbsp	oil *or* **3 Tbsp** butter, softened
¼ tsp	kosher salt
¼ cup	extra-mini chocolate chips

1. Preheat oven to 375°F. Line a 12-cup muffin pan with paper liners.

2. **Prepare the streusel topping:** In a medium bowl, combine topping ingredients, mixing with a fork. Set aside.

3. **Prepare the banana caramel muffins:** In a large bowl, mash bananas. Stir in lemon juice. Add all remaining muffin ingredients. Whisk until smooth. Do not overmix.

4. Fill each muffin cup halfway with batter. Microwave the caramel sauce for 20 seconds so it pours easily. Drop about 1 teaspoon sauce into the center of the batter in each cup. Top with remaining batter, filling each muffin cup almost to the top.

5. Sprinkle each muffin with 1 tablespoon streusel topping.

6. Bake 25-30 minutes, until set and golden.

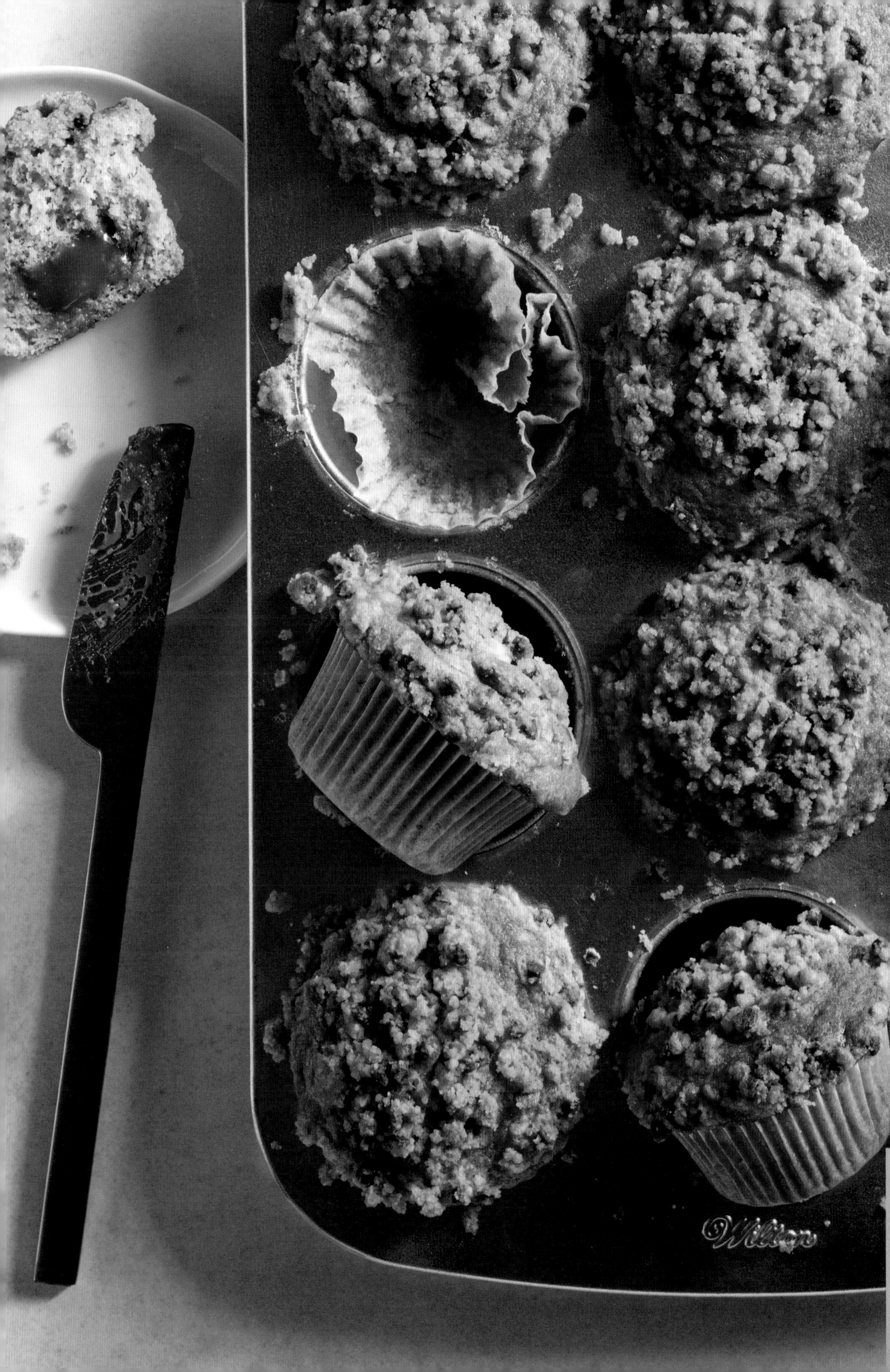
Wilton

Salads

HOW DO YOU DRESS YOUR SALAD?

Pareve

YIELDS *vary*

Here are a few of my salad dressing staples.

RED WINE VINAIGRETTE

¼ **cup**	red wine vinegar
¼ **cup**	honey
¼ **cup**	sugar
¼ **cup**	olive oil
1 Tbsp	Dijon mustard
1 tsp	sea salt
⅓ **tsp**	coarsely ground black pepper
1 Tbsp	poppy seeds

This vinaigrette is a beautifully balanced dressing that can work well with any salad... simply perfect!

» Place ingredients into a cruet or small bowl. Shake vigorously or whisk until emulsified and combined.

BLACKBERRY SHALLOT DRESSING

¼ **cup**	blackberry preserves (see Note)
1 Tbsp	Dijon mustard
1 Tbsp	lemon juice
1 small	shallot, chopped
1 clove	garlic
¼ **cup**	balsamic vinegar
•	sea salt, to taste
•	black pepper, to taste
½ **cup**	olive oil

Fabulous with a leafy salad as well as a quinoa-based salad, this subtle fruit flavoring pairs well with virtually any salad.

1. Place all ingredients, except olive oil, into a food processor fitted with the S-blade. Pulse to blend. While it is blending, slowly add olive oil until creamy and emulsified.

2. Alternatively, this can be done with an immersion blender in a bowl or tall container.

— Note —

Substitute blackberry preserves with red currant jelly or raspberry jam for a slightly different flavor.

CREAMY SCALLION AND GARLIC DRESSING

1 cup	mayonnaise
1 clove	garlic
3	scallions, white and light green parts only
¼ cup	dried parsley flakes
1½ Tbsp	lemon juice
1 Tbsp	vinegar
¼ tsp	sea salt
•	black pepper, to taste

This dressing is a winner that will make almost any salad (except a fruity one) a home run!

1. Place all ingredients into a food processor fitted with the S-blade. Pulse to blend.

2. Alternatively, this can be done with an immersion blender in a bowl or tall container.

GAIL'S RASPBERRY VINAIGRETTE

⅔ cup	frozen raspberries, thawed
½ cup	sugar
¼ cup	red wine vinegar
1 Tbsp	ground mustard
½ tsp	sea salt
1 Tbsp	lemon juice
1 Tbsp	poppy seeds, optional
1 cup	olive oil

This is the perfect complement to any fruity salad.

1. Place all ingredients, except olive oil, into a food processor fitted with the S-blade. Pulse to blend. While it is blending, slowly add olive oil until creamy and emulsified.

2. Alternatively, this can be done with an immersion blender in a bowl or tall container.

ALL-AROUND-PERFECT DRESSING

3 Tbsp	sugar
¼ tsp	ground mustard
3 cloves	garlic
1 tsp	sea salt
½ tsp	dried oregano
½ tsp	coarsely ground black pepper
⅓ cup	vinegar
1-2 Tbsp	mayonnaise
1 cup	canola oil

This dressing works beautifully in any salad and is also a fabulous topping to a salad with fish, meat, or grilled chicken.

1. Place all ingredients, except canola oil, into a food processor fitted with the S-blade. Pulse to blend. While it is blending, slowly add olive oil until creamy and emulsified. Run the food processor for 5-8 minutes to whip the dressing to perfection.

2. Alternatively, this can be done with an immersion blender in a bowl or tall container.

CREAMY DILL SLAW

Pareve   YIELDS *8 servings*

Whether you like to prepare in advance or are a last-minute person, this updated twist on the typical slaw is a great choice. It is delicious right away, and equally so after marinating in the fridge. You might want to consider doubling the recipe so you can enjoy on Shabbos and beyond.

14 oz	shredded green cabbage
½ cup	shelled pumpkin seeds
½ cup	dried cranberries
½ cup	sliced red onion
1	red pepper, sliced into 1-inch matchsticks

Creamy Dill Dressing

1¼ cups	mayonnaise
¼ cup	nondairy milk + **3 Tbsp** lemon juice
⅓ cup	fresh dill leaves (stems discarded) *or* **4 cubes** frozen dill
¼ small	onion, sliced
3 cloves	garlic, crushed
2	baby dill gherkins, diced
3 Tbsp	dill gherkin liquid
½ tsp	sea salt

1. **Prepare the dill dressing:** In a small bowl, puree dressing ingredients with an immersion blender. Alternatively, place all ingredients into a food processor fitted with the S-blade. Pulse until smooth.

2. Set aside half the dressing for the slaw. Refrigerate remaining dressing for future use.

3. In a large bowl, combine salad components. Stir in prepared dressing.

ZISI'S "DOWN UNDER" TOMATO SALAD

Pareve · YIELDS 4-6 servings

1 pint grape tomatoes, halved
2 Tbsp mayonnaise
2 cloves garlic, crushed
  • salt, to taste
  • black pepper, to taste

My Australian daughter-in-law Zisi introduced me to her favorite salad from Down Under. Whenever she comes for Shabbos, everyone requests Zisi's Tomato Salad. This flavor-packed salad with just a few ingredients is one I am sure you will love, too.

1. In a medium bowl, combine mayonnaise, garlic, salt, and black pepper.

2. Add tomatoes. Toss to coat.

Variation

Use multicolored grape tomatoes to add color to your table.

CHARRED CORN SALAD

Pareve YIELDS *6-8 servings*

6 ears corn
2 Tbsp olive oil
½ Tbsp garlic salt
½ Tbsp lemon pepper

Dressing

2 Tbsp mayonnaise
1 Tbsp olive oil
2 Tbsp lime juice
1 clove garlic, crushed
1 tsp sea salt
½ tsp coarsely ground black pepper

While shooting the photo for this salad, my friend and food stylist, Renee, marveled at how we were able to achieve such gorgeous charring on the corn without using a grill. After a sneak peek, taste testing, and recipe sharing, it has now become a staple in her home.

1. Preheat oven to 400°F. Line a baking sheet with parchment paper.

2. Place corn on prepared baking sheet. Drizzle with olive oil. Season with garlic salt and lemon pepper. Toss to combine and evenly coat each corn ear.

3. Bake 30-35 minutes, turning after 15 minutes. Allow corn to cool completely.

4. **Meanwhile, prepare the dressing:** In a small bowl, whisk together all dressing ingredients. Set aside.

5. Slice corn kernels from the cob. Pour dressing over corn; toss to combine.

Note

Ears of corn can be substituted with 2 (15-oz) cans corn. Drain corn, place on paper towels or clean kitchen towel and lightly rub to dry kernels. Proceed with above directions, but reduce baking time to 15 minutes. Be sure to use a metal baking sheet for optimal char.

RAIZEL'S FAVORITE QUINOA SALAD

Pareve   YIELDS *6 servings*

I was hosting a function in my home, and Raizel brought this salad. It was a resounding hit! Wholesome and filling, this versatile salad can be paired with any main and is terrific all on its own. Thank you, Raizel H., for graciously allowing me to share it here.

1 small	butternut squash, peeled and cubed
1½ Tbsp	olive oil
•	kosher salt, to taste
•	black pepper, to taste
1 cup	quinoa, prepared according to package directions
4-5 oz	fresh spinach, sliced thinly
1	avocado, peeled and diced
⅓ cup	dried cranberries
•	fresh basil, optional

Sweet and Savory Vinaigrette

4 Tbsp	red wine vinegar
2 Tbsp	pure maple syrup
1½ Tbsp	Dijon mustard
½ tsp	dried oregano
1 tsp	dried basil
1 clove	garlic, crushed
½ cup	olive oil
3 Tbsp	lemon juice

1. Preheat oven to 425°F. Line a baking pan with parchment paper.

2. Toss squash cubes with olive oil, salt, and pepper. Place on prepared baking pan. Roast for 15 minutes. Toss cubes; roast an additional 20 minutes, until tender.

3. In a large serving bowl, combine quinoa, roasted squash, spinach, avocado, cranberries, and basil.

4. **Prepare the sweet and savory vinaigrette:** In a small bowl, whisk together vinaigrette ingredients.

5. Pour vinaigrette over salad; mix well.

— Tip
To expedite the process when slicing the fresh spinach, pile 10 leaves on top of each other and then cut through them together.

BROILED PEPPER AND MUSHROOM SALAD

Pareve   YIELDS *4-6 servings*

It's no secret that I love mushrooms. So much so, I often have an overabundance on hand. The inspiration for this salad is the result of one of those occasions.

1 red pepper, thinly sliced

1 yellow pepper, thinly sliced

1 orange pepper, thinly sliced

16 oz baby bella mushrooms, sliced

¼ cup pine nuts, toasted (see Note)

• fresh parsley *or* basil, optional, for garnish

Dressing

6 Tbsp olive oil

4½ Tbsp rice vinegar

1½ tsp kosher salt

½ tsp coarsely ground black pepper

9 cloves garlic, crushed, *or* **9 cubes** frozen garlic

1½ Tbsp dried basil *or* **1 cube** frozen basil

1. Preheat oven to broil. Prepare a baking sheet and a 9x13-inch baking pan.

2. **Prepare the dressing:** In a small bowl, combine dressing ingredients. Whisk well.

3. Toss sliced peppers with 2-3 tablespoons dressing. Spread peppers on prepared baking sheet.

4. Place mushrooms in prepared pan. Pour half the remaining dressing into pan; toss to coat.

5. Place baking sheet on the center rack and mushroom pan on the lower rack. Broil 5 minutes. Toss peppers; broil an additional 3-5 minutes, until edges of peppers are beginning to char. Remove peppers from oven; set aside to cool. Toss cooled peppers with remaining dressing.

6. Stir mushrooms; move pan to center rack. Broil an additional 5 minutes; remove from oven.

7. Combine peppers and mushrooms. Toss to combine. Top with toasted pine nuts. If desired, toss with fresh parsley or basil.

— Note

To toast pine nuts, bake for 5 minutes at 350°F, or toast in a skillet over medium heat for a few minutes.

THE UPPER CRUST SWEET POTATO SALAD

Dairy   YIELDS *4 servings*

The Upper Crust is a dairy restaurant in my hometown of Lakewood, NJ. We frequent it often because the food is consistently delicious. This salad is sure to be on our order and is a real favorite in our family. Special shout-out to owner Shloime Green for sharing his most popular salad!

2	sweet potatoes, peeled
2-3 Tbsp	olive oil
1 tsp	kosher salt
¼ tsp	coarsely ground black pepper
1 tsp	garlic powder
1	red pepper
8 oz	lettuce of choice
1	red onion, sliced
½ cup	honey-glazed almond slivers
¾ cup	feta cheese, shaved

Creamy Balsamic Dressing

1 cup	mayonnaise
2 Tbsp	balsamic vinegar
2¼ tsp	light brown sugar
1 tsp	Dijon mustard
½ tsp	sea salt
⅛ tsp	coarsely ground black pepper

1. Preheat oven to 300°F. Line a baking sheet with parchment paper.

2. Cut sweet potatoes into shoestring fries; place into a bowl. Add olive oil, salt, pepper, and garlic powder. Toss to coat. Place on prepared baking sheet in a single layer. Bake, covered, for 30-35 minutes. (For a crispier texture, take out of the oven after 22 minutes and fry in oil at 325°F.)

3. Meanwhile, place red pepper over flame; rotate until mostly charred. Place in a covered pot for 20-30 minutes. Peel pepper; cut into thin slices.

4. **Prepare the dressing:** In a small bowl, whisk together dressing ingredients.

5. **To assemble:** In a large salad bowl or on individual plates, arrange lettuce, pepper, onion, sweet potatoes, and almonds. Drizzle with dressing. Top with feta cheese.

— Note

Short on time? You can skip roasting the red pepper and substitute store-bought jarred roasted red peppers.

HOUSE SALAD WITH PARMESAN CROUTONS

Dairy or Pareve

YIELDS *4-6 servings*

8 oz	spring mix, summer crisp, or lettuce of choice
1	avocado, diced
1 cup	prepared chickpeas (see Note)
1 cup	grape tomatoes, halved
1 medium	Persian cucumber, sliced into thin rounds
1	red or yellow pepper, cut into 1-inch matchsticks
½ cup	shredded mozzarella cheese

House Dressing

1 cup	mayonnaise
2 Tbsp	olive oil
2 Tbsp	sugar
2 Tbsp	pure maple syrup
1 Tbsp	vinegar
¼ tsp	sea salt
¼ tsp	coarsely ground black pepper
¼ tsp	dried basil
¼ tsp	garlic powder

Parmesan Croutons

2 Tbsp	margarine *or* butter
3 Tbsp	olive oil
4 cups	cubed sourdough *or* any hard-crusted bread such as ciabatta or French
½ Tbsp	garlic powder
½ Tbsp	onion powder
1 Tbsp	dried parsley flakes
2 Tbsp	grated Parmesan cheese

Here is a perfect example of a simple salad becoming simply spectacular. With the addition of the delicious dressing and homemade Parmesan croutons, this is a true standout.

1. **Prepare the house dressing:** Combine dressing ingredients in a small bowl. Whisk until smooth and creamy.

2. **Prepare the Parmesan croutons:** In a large skillet, over medium heat, melt margarine and oil. Add bread; toss until cubes are coated. Fry until light and golden on each side. Remove from heat. Toss croutons with spices and Parmesan cheese to evenly coat.

3. **To assemble:** Combine all vegetables in a large salad bowl. Add shredded cheese. Top with croutons. Drizzle with dressing. Toss and enjoy!

Notes

These croutons are best fresh but can be stored in an airtight container until needed. Nothing beats fresh croutons, but if you are short on time, store-bought croutons are a good substitute.

I use prepared chick peas from the grocery's refrigerated section.

Variation

For a pareve option, omit mozzarella and Parmesan cheeses.

HONEY-MUSTARD KALE SALAD

Pareve   YIELDS *6 servings*

"Sweet and tart with a great crunch" describes this salad to a T. When the kale is tossed with crisp, juicy apples, toasted pecans, cranberries, and honey-mustard dressing, the results are simply epic.

8 oz	prepared colored or green kale, sliced thinly (see Note)
1 small	Honeycrisp or Pink Lady apple, cored and julienned to 1-inch matchsticks
1 small	red onion, finely diced
small	handful toasted pecan halves
⅓ cup	dried cranberries

Honey-Mustard Dressing

¼ cup	olive oil
¼ cup	honey
2 Tbsp	yellow mustard
2 Tbsp	lemon juice
½ tsp	sea salt
¼ tsp	coarsely ground black pepper
2-3 cloves	garlic, crushed

1. **Prepare the honey-mustard dressing:** In a medium bowl, whisk together dressing ingredients until completely combined.

2. Place kale into a serving bowl. Add apple, onion, pecans, and cranberries. Drizzle with dressing. Toss to combine.

— Note

Massage the kale leaves with olive oil to soften.

ROASTED BROCCOLI AND CAULIFLOWER SALAD

Pareve YIELDS *6-8 servings*

When broccoli and cauliflower are roasted until perfectly tender and crisp, my family literally cannot get enough. This salad utilizes the ever-popular duo in a unique way and is sure to become a go-to for you.

8 oz	spring lettuce mix
1	Persian cucumber, sliced
1	yellow pepper, cut into 1-inch matchsticks
1 cup	grape tomatoes, halved
4 oz	shredded red cabbage
1	avocado, sliced
2 Tbsp	shelled sunflower seeds
2 Tbsp	shelled pumpkin seeds
2 Tbsp	shelled pistachios

Roasted Vegetables

16 oz	broccoli, fresh or frozen
16 oz	cauliflower, fresh or frozen
¼ cup	olive oil
1 tsp	kosher salt
¼ tsp	coarsely ground black pepper
3-4 Tbsp	balsamic vinegar *or* balsamic reduction (see Note)

Light Poppy Vinaigrette

5 Tbsp	olive oil
¼ cup	honey
3 Tbsp	apple cider vinegar
½ tsp	poppy seeds
½ tsp	dried mustard
½ tsp	sea salt

1. Preheat oven to 400°F. Line 2 baking sheets with parchment paper; coat with cooking spray.

2. Spread broccoli evenly over one baking sheet and cauliflower over the second. Drizzle olive oil over vegetables on each baking sheet. Sprinkle with kosher salt and black pepper. Drizzle with balsamic vinegar. Toss to combine.

3. Place both pans into the oven; roast for 20 minutes. Switch position of the pans; roast for an additional 10 minutes. Remove from oven; allow to cool slightly.

4. **Prepare the light poppy vinaigrette:** In a small bowl, whisk together vinaigrette ingredients until thickened. Set aside.

5. **To assemble:** Arrange lettuce, cucumber, pepper, tomatoes, cabbage, and avocado in a large salad bowl or on a platter, as pictured. Top with roasted vegetables. Drizzle with vinaigrette; toss salad. Top with seeds and nuts.

— Note

To make balsamic reduction, bring 1 cup balsamic vinegar to a boil in a small saucepan. low boil for 15 minutes. Remove from heat; stir in 2 tablespoons powdered sugar. Allow to cool before using.

FRUITY SPINACH SALAD

Pareve   YIELDS *6 servings*

Colorful and sweet, this salad is brimming with nature's summer bounty. It is truly as tasty as it is beautiful.

8 oz	baby spinach leaves
1 (8-oz) can	mandarin orange segments, drained
1 cup	blueberries
2 cups	fresh strawberries, cleaned and quartered
1 small	red onion, sliced

Candied Walnuts

1 cup	walnut halves
3 Tbsp	sugar

Dressing

⅓ cup	extra light olive oil
3 Tbsp	red wine vinegar
2 Tbsp	sugar
2 Tbsp	dried parsley flakes
1 tsp	Dijon mustard
1 clove	garlic, crushed
½ tsp	sea salt
⅛ tsp	coarsely ground black pepper

1. **Prepare the candied walnuts:** Set out a sheet of parchment paper or foil. Place walnut halves and sugar into a small saucepan; set over medium-low heat. Wait for the sugar to start melting. (Watch carefully so the sugar doesn't burn.) When the sugar begins to turn a light amber color, stir to coat all the walnuts. Transfer mixture to prepared parchment paper. Set aside to cool and set.

2. **Prepare the dressing:** Whisk together all dressing ingredients in a small bowl until well combined.

3. **To assemble:** Arrange spinach, oranges, blueberries, strawberries, and red onion in a large bowl or on individual plates. Pour dressing over salad; toss. Top with candied walnuts.

— Note

For dairy meals, this salad pairs beautifully with crumbled feta, fresh goat cheese, or fresh mozzarella cheese.

HONEY-LIME NUT SALAD

Pareve   YIELDS *6 servings*

Nothing speaks louder than an empty bowl. Whenever I make this spectacular salad, every bite is gone. These nuts are a little sweet, a little salty, a little spicy, and a lot a delicious. I would be remiss in not relaying the fabulousness of the dressing too. Make sure to double both!

8 oz	romaine lettuce
1	avocado, diced
1 cup	grape tomatoes, halved
½	red onion, sliced
1½ cups	Sweet 'n Spicy Nut Mix

Sweet 'N Spicy Nut Mix

1 cup	raw cashews
1 cup	raw pecan halves
½ cup	raw almonds
¼ cup	pine nuts
1 Tbsp	margarine, melted
1 Tbsp	maple syrup
¾ tsp	kosher salt
½ tsp	vanilla extract
⅛ tsp	cayenne pepper, or to taste

Honey-Lime Dressing

¼ cup	canola oil
2 Tbsp	honey
2 Tbsp	apple cider vinegar
1 Tbsp	lime juice
1 Tbsp	diced onions
¼ tsp	ground mustard
¼ tsp	sea salt

1. Preheat oven to 325°F. Line a baking sheet with parchment paper.

2. **Prepare the sweet 'n spicy nut mix:** In a large bowl, combine nuts. Toss with melted margarine, maple syrup, salt, vanilla, and cayenne pepper. Mix until evenly coated. Transfer mixture to prepared baking sheet in a single layer.

3. Bake for 10 minutes on center rack. Stir; bake an additional 15 minutes. Remove from oven; stir again. Spread mixture into an even layer to cool. The coating will harden as it cools.

4. **Prepare the honey-lime dressing:** In a small bowl or container, combine dressing ingredients. Pulse with an immersion blender to combine. Alternatively, this can be done in a food processor fitted with the S-blade.

5. **To assemble:** Place lettuce, avocados, tomatoes, onion, and cooled nuts into a large serving bowl. Drizzle with honey-lime dressing. Toss and enjoy!

— Note

This nut mix is so spectacular, it is also amazing on its own as a snack, not only in a salad.

SIMPLE SUPPER

GRILLED CHICKEN CAESAR SALAD

Meat   YIELDS *8 servings*

Classic Caesar salad gets a flavor facelift, thanks to the herb-marinated chicken and the fabulous dressing! This is a fuss-free weeknight meal and perfect for a Shabbos or Yom Tov appetizer, too. Double the dressing to use on other salads ... yes, it is that good.

1 lb	chicken cutlets
12 oz	lettuce of choice
½	red onion, sliced
1 cup	grape tomatoes, halved

Herb Marinade

2 Tbsp	olive oil
2 Tbsp	lemon juice
3 cloves	garlic, crushed
½ tsp	dried oregano
½ tsp	dried basil

Caesar Dressing

¾ cup	mayonnaise
2 cloves	garlic, crushed
3 Tbsp	sugar
2 Tbsp	vinegar
1½ Tbsp	water

1. **Prepare the herb marinade:** Combine marinade ingredients in a large resealable bag.

2. Add chicken to bag; marinate for at least 15 minutes or overnight in the fridge.

3. Preheat grill pan over medium-high heat. Remove pan from heat; coat with cooking spray. Return to heat.

4. Grill each cutlet for 3-4 minutes per side. Discard any remaining marinade. Remove from pan; set aside to cool. Cut chicken into strips.

5. **Prepare the Caesar dressing:** In a medium measuring cup, whisk together dressing ingredients until smooth.

6. **To assemble:** Arrange lettuce on plates. Add red onion and grape tomatoes. Top with chicken strips. Drizzle with dressing.

GRILLED SKIRT STEAK SALAD

Meat   YIELDS *4-6 servings*

Whether on its own as a simple supper or as the star of this salad, this skirt steak is bursting with flavor. The result, when combined with the lemon-pesto dressing and salad components, is simply superb.

8 oz	lettuce of choice
1	avocado, sliced
½ cup	prepared chickpeas
1 cup	grape tomatoes, halved
½ cup	shelled sunflower seeds

Skirt Steak

2 lb	skirt steak
2 Tbsp	low sodium soy sauce
3 cloves	garlic, crushed
2 Tbsp	light brown sugar

Lemon-Pesto Dressing

5 Tbsp	prepared pesto, store-bought or homemade (page 100)
3 Tbsp	olive oil
•	zest of 1 lemon
1 Tbsp	lemon juice
1½ tsp	Dijon mustard
¼ tsp	garlic salt
¼ tsp	coarsely ground black pepper

1. **Prepare the skirt steak:** Place skirt steak into a bowl. Add water to cover. Allow to soak for 10 minutes to remove the saltiness. Pour off water; pat meat dry. Cut meat into 4-inch pieces.

2. In a small cup, combine soy sauce, garlic, and brown sugar.

3. Preheat oven to broil. Coat a baking sheet with cooking spray.

4. Place meat on prepared baking sheet. Brush soy sauce mixture over the meat; marinate at room temperature for 10 minutes. Broil for 10-12 minutes on the upper rack of oven.

5. Let meat rest for 5 minutes. Cut into slices across the grain.

6. **Prepare the lemon-pesto dressing:** In a bowl or container, whisk together dressing ingredients.

7. Combine salad ingredients. Top with skirt steak. Drizzle with lemon-pesto dressing.

GREEN GOODNESS

Pareve   YIELDS *vary*

My Shabbos table just isn't complete without an assortment of dips. These three dips are constants and plain and simple green goodness. I couldn't resist including my homemade pesto, which I utilize in so many ways, as seen in this cookbook.

HOMEMADE PESTO

2 cups   fresh basil leaves, packed, *or* **20 cubes** frozen basil

¾ cup   olive oil

1½ tsp   sea salt

1 tsp   coarsely ground black pepper

4 cloves   garlic

1. Combine pesto ingredients in a small bowl or tall container. Pulse with an immersion blender until a smooth consistency is reached.

2. Alternatively, place all ingredients into a food processor fitted with the S-blade. Pulse until smooth.

PESTO DIP

1 cup   mayonnaise

½ cup   prepared pesto, homemade or store-bought

¼ tsp   garlic powder

» In a small bowl, combine mayonnaise, pesto, and garlic powder. Whisk to combine.

DILL DIP

1 cup	mayonnaise
1 cup	fresh dill leaves, stems discarded, *or* **4-6 cubes** frozen dill
¼ cup	prepared white horseradish
1 Tbsp	lemon juice
½ tsp	sea salt
¼ tsp	coarsely ground black pepper
2 Tbsp	sugar, optional

1. Combine ingredients in a small bowl or tall container. Pulse with an immersion blender until a smooth consistency is reached.

2. Alternatively, place all ingredients into a food processor fitted with the S-blade. Pulse until smooth.

ROASTED GARLIC JALAPEÑO DIP

4	jalapeño peppers, halved and seeded
2 heads	garlic
3 Tbsp	olive oil, divided
•	kosher salt, to taste
•	black pepper, to taste
1 cup	mayonnaise
2 Tbsp	sugar
2 Tbsp	lime juice
½ tsp	kosher salt

— Tip —

This recipe can easily be doubled!

1. Preheat oven to 400°F. Coat a small pan with cooking spray. Prepare 2 pieces of aluminum foil, each large enough to wrap a garlic head.

2. Place jalapeño halves into prepared pan. Drizzle with 1 tablespoon olive oil; season with salt and pepper. Cut off the tops of the garlic heads to expose the cloves. Place each head of garlic on prepared foil. Pour 1 tablespoon olive oil over each garlic head. Season with kosher salt and pepper. Seal foil; add to pan.

3. Bake for 30 minutes. Remove from oven; allow to cool.

4. Push the garlic cloves from the head into a tall container by pushing upward from the bottom. Add roasted jalapeños, mayonnaise, sugar, lime juice, and kosher salt. Puree with an immersion blender. This dip will stay fresh for 2 weeks in the refrigerator.

Soups

SAVORY SWEET POTATO SOUP

Pareve YIELDS *8 servings*

This velvety smooth, satisfying soup has just the right amount of sweetness, with a welcome savory twist.

2 Tbsp	margarine
2 Tbsp	olive oil
2 medium	yellow onions, diced
3 cloves	garlic, crushed
1½ Tbsp	kosher salt, divided
3-4 ribs	celery (1 cup sliced)
2 small	carrots, peeled and sliced
4 medium	sweet potatoes, peeled and cubed
8 cups	water
1 tsp	dried basil
¾ tsp	ground ginger
½ tsp	coarsely ground black pepper

1. In an 8-quart pot, over medium heat, melt margarine and olive oil. Add onions; sauté, stirring frequently, until soft and translucent, about 10 minutes.

2. Add garlic and 1 tablespoon salt. Stir to combine. Add celery, carrots, and sweet potatoes. Sauté for 2-3 minutes. Add water; season with remaining 1 tablespoon salt, basil, ginger, and black pepper.

3. Bring to a boil. Reduce heat; cover and simmer over low heat for 25 minutes, until vegetables are very tender.

4. Using an immersion blender, puree the soup until smooth and creamy.

— Note

This soup is freezer friendly.

QUICK BROCCOLI BISQUE

Pareve YIELDS *8 servings*

As I was trying to troubleshoot for all those hard-working people with limited time, this easy and versatile soup came into being. Without compromising flavor — done!

2-3 Tbsp	olive oil
2	leeks, white and light green parts only, sliced
1 rib	celery, sliced
3 cloves	garlic, crushed
3 cups	water
36 oz	fresh or frozen broccoli
2 Tbsp	kosher salt
½ tsp	coarsely ground black pepper
⅛ tsp	nutmeg
3 cups	nondairy milk

1. Heat oil in an 8-quart stock pot. Add leeks, celery, and garlic; sauté until tender, about 10 minutes. Add water, broccoli, salt, pepper, and nutmeg. Bring to a boil over medium-high heat. Reduce heat. Cover; simmer for 10 minutes.

2. Using an immersion blender, puree soup. Return to heat; add nondairy milk. Stir until thick and bubbly. Simmer for 5 minutes. Adjust seasoning if necessary.

— Note ———————————————

This soup is freezer friendly.

WHITE BEAN SOUP

Meat or Pareve

YIELDS *8 servings*

¼ cup	olive oil
4 oz	portobello mushrooms, diced
1 oz	dried porcini mushrooms, reconstituted (see Note), squeezed totally dry, and diced (optional, but recommended)
3 large	shallots, diced
2 medium	onions, diced
6 cloves	garlic, crushed
3 ribs	celery, diced
2	parsnips, peeled and diced
1	yellow squash, peeled and diced
½ tsp	dried crushed rosemary
2 (15-oz) cans	small white beans, rinsed and drained
6 cups	chicken broth *or* **6 cups** water + **2 Tbsp** consommé powder
2	bay leaves
1 Tbsp	kosher salt
1 tsp	coarsely ground black pepper

My parents were coming for Shabbos and my mother requested a pareve soup with protein. To keep it protein packed, I chose beans and added mushrooms for depth. The rave reviews were overwhelming. Thanks for the inspiration, Ema!

1. In an 8-quart pot, heat olive oil over medium heat. Add diced mushrooms; sauté for 3-5 minutes, until browned. Lower heat to medium-low. Add shallots, onions, garlic, celery, parsnips, squash, and rosemary. Cook for 10 minutes, until the vegetables are tender.

2. Add beans, broth, bay leaves, salt, and pepper. Bring to a boil. Lower heat; simmer for 45 minutes, partially covered. Stir occasionally.

3. Discard bay leaves before serving.

Note

To reconstitute dried mushrooms, steep mushrooms in boiling water for 15-20 minutes.

Variation

For a great meat option, you can substitute beef fry for the dried porcini mushrooms. Dice 6 ounces beef fry. In Step 1, sauté beef fry in the olive oil until crispy. Remove with slotted spoon; set aside. Continue with Step 1 (omitting the porcini mushrooms). Add crisped beef fry to soup before serving.

SILKY ASPARAGUS SOUP

Pareve YIELDS *6 servings*

Looking for a tasty way to get your healthy greens? Look no further. This combination of asparagus and zucchini is flavor-packed and pureed to silky perfection.

3 Tbsp	olive oil
1 large	onion, diced
5 large	shallots, diced
4 cloves	garlic, crushed
3-4 Tbsp	kosher salt, divided
¾-1 tsp	coarsely ground black pepper, divided
6 small	zucchini, 3 peeled and 3 unpeeled, cubed
1 lb	frozen asparagus, chopped
6 cups	water
2 Tbsp	lemon juice

1. In a large pot, over medium-high heat, heat oil. Add onion, shallots, garlic, 1 tablespoon salt, and a pinch of pepper. Cook, stirring frequently, until soft and translucent (about 8 minutes). Add zucchini and asparagus. Add water and remaining salt and pepper. Bring to a boil. Cover pot, reduce heat, and simmer for 30 minutes.

2. Use an immersion blender to puree soup until completely smooth. Stir in lemon juice. Taste; adjust seasoning if necessary.

— Note

This soup is freezer friendly.

VELVETY MUSHROOM LEEK SOUP

Pareve   YIELDS *8 servings*

As a self-proclaimed and unabashed mushroom lover, I proudly say this is one of my all-time favorites. The creamy, velvety texture has a depth of flavor that is outstanding. Coupled with roasted garlic in a creamy base, the earthy mushroom tones make this the epitome of a true mushroom experience.

1 head	garlic
4 Tbsp	olive oil, divided
•	sea salt, to taste
•	black pepper, to taste
24 oz	shiitake mushrooms, *or* mushroom of choice, sliced
3 Tbsp	kosher salt, divided
2	leeks, white and light green parts only, washed and sliced
4 large	shallots, thinly sliced
½ tsp	coarsely ground black pepper + more for garnish, optional
1 tsp	umami powder, optional
1 Tbsp	balsamic vinegar
4 cups	water
4 cups	nondairy milk

Crispy Mushroom Croutons

3½ oz	shiitake mushrooms *or* mushroom of choice, sliced
2 Tbsp	olive oil
•	kosher salt, to taste
•	black pepper, to taste
2 Tbsp	teriyaki sauce

1. Preheat oven to 350°F. Prepare a small piece of foil.

2. Slice off and discard the top of the head of garlic. Place garlic head in the center of prepared foil. Drizzle with 1 tablespoon olive oil; sprinkle with sea salt and pepper to taste. Seal foil around garlic; place in a muffin tin or a pan. Bake for 30 minutes.

3. In an 8-quart pot, over medium-high heat, heat remaining 3 tablespoons olive oil. Add mushrooms; stir until they release their moisture. Raise heat; stir until most of the moisture is absorbed. Add 1 tablespoon salt, stirring to combine. Stir in leeks and shallots.

4. Pop out the roasted garlic cloves by pushing upward from the bottom of the head. Add garlic to the pot. Stir; cook for 7 minutes. Add remaining 2 tablespoons salt, black pepper, and umami powder, if using. Stir in balsamic vinegar, water, and nondairy milk. Allow soup to reach a low boil. Reduce heat; simmer for 20 minutes.

5. **Meanwhile, prepare the mushroom croutons:** In a 1-quart pot over medium heat, heat olive oil. Add mushrooms. Let mushrooms sweat for 3-4 minutes until they release their liquid. Sprinkle with salt and pepper. Raise heat; stir mushrooms until all liquid is absorbed and mushrooms are slightly crispy. Add teriyaki sauce; stir until completely combined. Set aside.

6. Remove soup pot from heat. Use an immersion blender to puree soup. Sprinkle with additional black pepper, if desired, to garnish. Top with mushroom croutons.

— Note

This soup is freezer friendly.

CHUNKY ROOT VEGETABLE SOUP

Pareve   YIELDS *8 servings*

Wanting to stay true to tradition and keep it familiar, I was wary of too much change to this classic. The medley of unique vegetables makes this not your same-old-same-old. The addition of tomato juice gives it a kick without overwhelming the flavors. One bowl and you'll see what I mean.

3 Tbsp	olive oil
1 large	onion, diced
3 large	shallots, diced
4 cloves	garlic, crushed
1	sweet potato, peeled and diced
1	Japanese yam, peeled and diced
1	Yukon Gold potato, peeled and diced
1 small	butternut squash, peeled and diced
1	parsnip, peeled and diced
1	bay leaf
2 Tbsp	kosher salt
1 tsp	dried thyme
½ tsp	dried basil
½ tsp	coarsely ground black pepper
6 cups	water
2 cups	tomato juice
½ cup	fresh parsley
½ cup	fresh dill

1. In an 8-quart pot, over medium-high heat, heat oil. Add onion and shallots; sauté for 10 minutes, stirring occasionally, until softened. Add garlic; cook for 1 minute. Add remaining vegetables and seasonings. Place parsley and dill into a spice bag. Add to pot. Add remaining ingredients.

2. Bring soup to a boil. Reduce heat; simmer for 1 hour. Remove and discard bay leaf and spice bag before serving.

JANEY'S REFRESHING FRUIT SOUP

Pareve   YIELDS *6-8 servings*

Garnished with fresh fruit, this palate-pleasing puree base is great for an anytime meal starter or dessert.

1 (28-oz) can	peaches, with their liquid
1 (16-oz) bag	frozen strawberries
1 cup	water
½ package (¼ cup)	strawberry jello powder
¼ cup	lemon juice
•	sliced strawberries and lemons or limes, for garnish

1. Place peaches, strawberries, water, jello powder, and lemon juice into a blender. Puree.

2. Serve chilled. Float strawberry and lemon slices on soup in each bowl.

—Note
This soup is freezer friendly.

EASY CHEESY CAULIFLOWER SOUP

Dairy YIELDS *6 servings*

One week I found myself close to Shabbos when I suddenly realized that I had forgotten to make soup. Frantically, I threw together some of these ingredients and hoped for the best. The quick and easy results were amazing! I decided to switch things up, so I made this dairy version. It is rich and creamy with the perfect balance of flavors.

24 oz	fresh or frozen cauliflower florets
3 large	shallots, sliced
3 cloves	garlic, crushed
1 rib	celery, sliced
2½ cups	pareve broth, *or* **2½ cups** water + **2 tsp** consommé powder
1 Tbsp	kosher salt
¼ tsp	coarsely ground black pepper
2½ cups	milk
2 Tbsp	low sodium soy sauce
¾ tsp	ground mustard
1 tsp	hot sauce
1 (14-oz) package	cheese tortellini, prepared according to package directions
½ cup	heavy cream

1. In a 6-8-quart pot, stir together cauliflower, shallots, garlic, celery, and broth. Bring to a boil over medium-high heat. Reduce heat; cover. Simmer for 15 minutes.

2. Add salt, pepper, milk, soy sauce, ground mustard, and hot sauce. Stir to combine. Bring to a boil over medium heat. Cook, stirring, for 2 minutes. Reduce heat; simmer for 10 minutes.

3. Puree with an immersion blender.

4. Return soup pot to stove over medium-low heat. Place tortellini in a single layer in the soup. Cover pot. Cook for 4 minutes, stirring once per minute to prevent tortellini from sticking to each other. Stir in heavy cream.

Note

This soup is freezer friendly. Reheat over low heat.

MEATY MUSHROOM BARLEY SOUP

Meat YIELDS *6-8 servings*

With beef, barley, and vegetables, this soup is hearty enough to be a full meal. There's nothing more satisfying than a big, steaming bowl on a cold winter day.

3 Tbsp	olive oil, divided
1 lb	gourmet flanken on the bone
1 Tbsp	kosher salt + more to taste
·	black pepper, to taste
1 large	onion, diced
2 cloves	garlic, crushed
1 rib	celery, diced
24 oz	baby bella mushrooms, sliced
4 Tbsp	sherry cooking wine
½ cup	barley, rinsed
7 cups	water
2	bay leaves
4 Tbsp	low sodium soy sauce
1 tsp	umami powder, optional

1. Heat an 8-quart pot or Dutch oven over medium-high heat. Add 2 tablespoons oil. Season meat generously with salt and pepper. Sear meat until well browned on all sides (about 15 minutes). Transfer to a platter; set aside.

2. Lower heat to medium. Add remaining tablespoon olive oil, onion, garlic, and celery to the pot; sauté until tender (about 10 minutes). Add mushrooms with a sprinkle of salt and pepper. Cook, uncovered, until mushrooms are soft. Add sherry wine, raise heat, and cook until liquid reduces.

3. Return meat to the pot. Add water and bay leaves. Bring to a boil. Adjust heat to maintain a gentle simmer. Cover; cook for 1½ hours, until meat is tender.

4. Add barley, soy sauce, 1 tablespoon salt, and umami powder, if using. Continue to simmer for an additional 30-45 minutes.

5. Remove meat and bay leaves from the soup. Discard bay leaves. Cut meat from the bone, dice, and return to soup. If desired, season with additional salt and pepper to taste.

— Tip —

If reheating soup, you may need to add water, since the barley tends to absorb lots of liquid.

BEEF MINESTRONE SOUP

Meat **YIELDS** *8 servings*

Hearty and robust, this meal in a bowl is extraordinarily satisfying.

2 Tbsp	olive oil
1 large	onion, diced
1 lb	ground beef
1 tsp	kosher salt, divided
½ tsp	coarsely ground black pepper, divided
2	carrots, peeled and diced
2 ribs	celery, diced
1 large	zucchini, diced
2 cloves	garlic, crushed
4 cups	beef broth *or* **4 cups** water + **4 tsp** beef broth powder
1 (28-oz) can	crushed tomatoes
1 (14½-oz) can	fire roasted diced tomatoes, with their liquid
1 tsp	dried basil
1 tsp	dried oregano
½ tsp	dried thyme
2	bay leaves
1 cup	ditalini pasta, prepared according to package directions

1. In an 8-quart pot over medium heat, heat olive oil. Add onion, beef, ½ tsp salt, and ¼ tsp pepper. Sauté 5-8 minutes, stirring, until onions are soft and beef is no longer pink. While stirring, break apart large clumps of meat.

2. Add carrots, celery, zucchini, and garlic. Sauté for 3 minutes.

3. Add beef broth, crushed tomatoes, fire-roasted tomatoes, basil, oregano, thyme, and bay leaves. Stir to combine. Bring to a boil. Reduce heat. Cover; simmer for 1 hour.

4. Discard bay leaves. Add remaining salt and pepper. Add cooked pasta before serving.

Fish

BATTER-DIPPED TILAPIA

Pareve   YIELDS *4 servings*

Need dinner in a pinch? This quick fish dish with its pillowy exterior and lemony tartar sauce will still taste delicious even the second time around.

1-1½ lb	skinless tilapia fillets
½ cup	flour
½ cup	cornstarch
1 tsp	baking powder
1 tsp	baking soda
1 tsp	garlic powder
½ tsp	sea salt
½ tsp	coarsely ground black pepper
¼ tsp	cayenne pepper
1	egg
⅔ cup	cold beer
•	oil, for frying

Tartar Sauce

½ cup	mayonnaise
1 Tbsp	lemon juice
2 Tbsp	chopped capers *or* chopped dill pickles
1 Tbsp	fresh dill *or* **1 tsp** dried dill
½ tsp	Dijon mustard
•	kosher salt, to taste
•	black pepper, to taste

1. **Prepare the tartar sauce:** Combine tartar sauce ingredients in a small bowl. Whisk well. Set aside.

2. **Prepare the fish:** In a large bowl, whisk together all dry ingredients. Add egg and beer; whisk until combined. Set aside.

3. Add 2 inches oil to a small saucepan. Heat over medium-high heat until oil reaches 350°F. Lower heat to medium to maintain temperature at 350°F.

4. Meanwhile, cut fish into strips or nuggets; add to prepared batter. Stir to completely coat fish pieces. Place a few batter-dipped pieces of fish into the hot oil; do not crowd pan. Fry until lightly golden, about 30-60 seconds per side. Transfer to a paper towel-lined cooling rack to drain. Continue with remaining fish.

5. Serve alongside tartar sauce.

Variation
Tilapia can be substituted with turbot, fluke, or flounder.

SPINACH FLOUNDER ROLL-UPS

Pareve YIELDS *6 servings*

Be sure to double this savory spinach mixture. It is not only fantastic with flounder, but it's also delicious enjoyed as a Shabbos dip.

6	flounder fillets
8 oz	frozen chopped spinach, thawed and squeezed dry
½ cup	mayonnaise
3 cloves	garlic
1½ tsp	sea salt
1 small	red onion, sliced

1. Preheat oven to 350°F. Spray a 9x13-inch baking pan with cooking spray.

2. In a medium bowl, combine spinach, mayonnaise, garlic, and salt. Use an immersion blender to pulse until smooth. Alternatively, this can be done using a food processor.

3. Place red onion slices on the bottom of prepared baking pan.

4. If flounder slices are very large, cut them lengthwise down the seam.

5. Spread 1 tablespoon spinach mixture over each flounder fillet until coated. Roll up flounder from the wider end; hold closed with a toothpick. Place roll-ups over onions in prepared pan.

6. Spread remaining spinach mixture over the flounder roll-ups.

7. Bake, uncovered, on center rack for 20 minutes.

Variation

Flounder can be substituted with turbot, fluke, or tilapia.

Tip

An easy way to drain liquid from spinach: Place thawed spinach in the center of a paper towel or cheesecloth. Twist and squeeze to remove any remaining liquid.

BARRAMUNDI WITH CREAMY LEMON SAUCE

Dairy   YIELDS *4 servings*

4 slices	barramundi
•	sea salt, to taste
•	onion powder, to taste
•	garlic powder, to taste
•	paprika, to taste
4 Tbsp	butter, divided
1 small clove	garlic, crushed
1 Tbsp	lemon juice, preferably fresh
2 Tbsp	hot water + **½ tsp** consommé powder
2 Tbsp	heavy cream
•	lemon wedges, for garnish
•	parsley, for garnish
•	black pepper, for garnish

Are you fussy about fish? Barramundi's mild taste works perfectly in just about any white fish recipe. The simply uncomplicated combination of lemon, butter, and garlic will satisfy even your most finicky fish eaters.

1. Preheat oven to high broil.

2. In a small saucepan, over medium-low heat, melt 3 tablespoons butter. Add crushed garlic; cook until it becomes fragrant (about 30 seconds).

3. In a small bowl, whisk together lemon juice, water with consommé powder, and heavy cream. Stir mixture into butter and garlic. Bring sauce to a simmer. Cook 4-6 minutes, until sauce thickens.

4. Pat barramundi slices dry; place into a 9x13-inch baking dish. Season with spices. Place ¼ tablespoon butter onto the center of each slice. Broil on center rack for 4 minutes. Remove from oven.

5. Pour creamy lemon sauce over barramundi. Garnish with lemon wedges, parsley, and freshly ground black pepper. Serve warm.

─ Tip ─

To keep the butter from separating as the sauce thickens, stir it continuously over low heat (if the heat is too high, the butter may burn).

─ Variation ─

Barramundi can be substituted with turbot, fluke, flounder, or tilapia.

EVERYTHING BAGEL SPICED TURBOT

SIMPLE SUPPER

Dairy YIELDS *4 servings*

Turbot is a firm white fish with a fantastic mild flavor. Although it can be a bit pricey, it's naturally delicious and doesn't need much to take it over the top.

- **4** (3x3-inch) turbot fillets
- • everything bagel seasoning, to taste
- **pinch** paprika
- **pinch** sea salt
- **pinch** onion powder
- **pinch** garlic powder
- **4 Tbsp** butter
- • lemon slivers, for garnish, optional

1. Preheat oven to high broil. Spray a 9x13-inch pan with cooking spray.

2. Pat turbot dry; place into prepared pan. Evenly yet lightly coat turbot with everything bagel seasoning. Sprinkle very lightly with remaining spices. Place ½ tablespoon butter toward the top and another toward the bottom of each slice of turbot.

3. Broil for 7 minutes on center rack. Serve warm. Garnish with a sliver of lemon, if desired.

—Variation

Turbot can be substituted with fluke, flounder, or tilapia.

SEARED TUNA WITH WHITE WINE VINAIGRETTE

Pareve   YIELDS *4 servings*

These tuna steaks are quickly seared and cooked to medium-rare perfection. The subtlety that the light vinaigrette adds completes this restaurant-worthy fabulous fish.

4 tuna steaks

• kosher salt, to taste

• black pepper, to taste

4 tsp Dijon mustard

2 Tbsp black sesame seeds

2 Tbsp sesame seeds

White Wine Vinaigrette

1 Tbsp white wine vinegar

½ tsp Dijon mustard

pinch sea salt

pinch coarsely ground black pepper

2 Tbsp sesame oil

¼ cup olive oil

1. Pat tuna steaks dry. Sprinkle generously with salt and pepper. Allow steaks to stand at room temperature as you heat your pan.

2. Heat cast iron skillet or grill pan over medium-high heat. Once heated, spray with cooking spray.

3. Place steaks on pan; sear for 1 minutes per side. If the steaks are thinner, sear for less time to obtain a medium-rare center.

4. Transfer steaks to a serving bowl. Spread 1 tsp Dijon mustard over the top of each steak. Sprinkle black and white sesame seeds over the mustard.

5. **Prepare the vinaigrette:** To a small bowl, add ingredients in the order listed, whisking until combined and thickened.

6. Serve vinaigrette beside each tuna steak or drizzled on top.

GARLICKY CITRUS BRANZINO

Dairy YIELDS *6 servings*

Branzino is mild tasting and quite versatile. Enhanced with the classic combination of garlic and citrus flavors, this is perfect for a simple and healthy weeknight meal.

- **4** branzino fillets
- • kosher salt, to taste
- • black pepper, to taste
- **2 Tbsp** lemon-infused olive oil (see Note)
- **½ cup** garlic butter, divided (see Note)
- **3** scallions, light and green parts only, cut into rounds
- **3** shallots, sliced into rounds
- **1** lemon, sliced
- **2 slices** orange, peeled

1. Preheat oven to 450°F. Line a baking sheet with parchment paper; coat with cooking spray.

2. Pat fish dry; place on prepared baking sheet. Drizzle with infused olive oil. Sprinkle generously with salt and pepper.

3. In a medium skillet, over medium-low heat, melt ¼ cup garlic butter. Sauté scallions and shallots until translucent. Raise heat; sauté until golden. Add lemon and orange slices. Lower heat; simmer for a few minutes.

4. Divide remaining garlic butter between branzino pieces. Remove skillet from heat; divide garlic-citrus mixture evenly over the fish.

5. Bake 15 minutes on center rack.

Note

Lemon-infused olive oil can be substituted with olive oil and lemon zest.

To make your own garlic butter, combine ½ cup softened butter and 1 clove crushed garlic or 1 cube frozen garlic.

Variation

Branzino can be substituted with turbot, fluke, flounder, or tilapia.

SEA BASS WITH MANGO PEACH CHUTNEY

Pareve YIELDS *6 servings*

Sweet, tangy, with a hint of heat, this chutney is quite versatile. I have served it over chicken, as well, with rave reviews. Here it is perfectly paired with the mild, delicate, buttery flavor of my favorite fish, sea bass.

3 (1½-inch-thick) sea bass center cut fillets, cut in half

• kosher salt, to taste

• black pepper, to taste

1 scallion, finely chopped, for garnish, optional

Mango Peach Chutney

2 Tbsp canola oil

1 small red onion, diced

1 scallion, trimmed and sliced

1 jalapeño pepper, seeded and diced finely

¼ tsp ground ginger

¼ tsp cayenne pepper

1 cup peach preserves, see Note

1 mango, peeled, pitted, and diced

1 tsp sea salt

1. Preheat oven to 350°F. Prepare a baking pan.

2. Rinse fish; pat dry. Place into prepared pan. Season with salt and pepper. Bake, uncovered, for 20 minutes.

3. **Meanwhile, prepare the mango peach chutney:** In a small saucepan, heat oil. Add onion, scallion, and jalapeño; sauté for 3 minutes. Add ginger and cayenne. Cook for 1 minute. Add preserves, mango, and salt. Cook at a low boil for 15 minutes, until thickened.

4. **To serve:** Place a piece of sea bass on each plate. Spoon chutney over fish. Garnish with finely chopped scallion, if desired.

— Note

For apricot mango chutney, substitute peach preserves with apricot preserves.

CAULIFLOWER-CRUSTED SALMON

Pareve   YIELDS *6-8 servings*

I always prepare extra of this cauliflower-topped salmon, knowing that I will enjoy it again the following day. The show-stopping presentation, with the combined depth of flavors that work so well together, will have you, just like me, coming back to this recipe again and again.

6-8	(1½-inch-thick) salmon fillets
•	onion powder, to taste
•	garlic powder, to taste
•	sea salt, to taste
•	paprika, to taste
½ cup	Dill Dip *or* Roasted Garlic Jalapeño Dip (page 101)
3-4 Tbsp	silan

Cauliflower Crumble Topping

16 oz	riced cauliflower, fresh or frozen , defrosted and drained
3 cloves	garlic, crushed
2 Tbsp	low sodium soy sauce
1 Tbsp	parsley flakes
½ tsp	lemon pepper
¼ tsp	sea salt
⅛ tsp	cayenne pepper

1. Preheat oven to 350°F. Prepare a 9x13-inch baking pan.

2. **Prepare the cauliflower crumble topping:** In a large bowl, toss together cauliflower crumble ingredients. Place into prepared pan. Bake for 20 minutes. Remove from oven; cool for 10 minutes.

3. Preheat oven to 400°F. Line a baking sheet with parchment paper.

4. Place salmon fillets on prepared baking sheet. Season fish with seasonings. Spread a heaping tablespoon of dip over each salmon fillet. Drizzle with silan. Top with cauliflower mixture. Drizzle again with silan.

5. Bake for 15-18 minutes.

Note

Cauliflower Cumble Topping can be prepared up to 2 days in advance. Refrigerate in an airtight container after cooling until ready to use.

SIMPLY SAVORY SALMON

Pareve YIELDS *4-5 servings*

Don't be fooled by the simplicity of putting this together. With its fresh, light garlic and lemon flavors, it simply can't be beat.

4-5 (1¼-1½-inch-thick) salmon fillets

- sea salt, to taste
- onion powder, to taste
- garlic powder, to taste
- paprika, to taste

Marinade

4 Tbsp avocado or canola oil

4 cloves garlic, crushed

2 Tbsp fresh parsley, chopped, *or* **¾ Tbsp** dried parsley flakes

- zest of 1 lemon
- juice of 1 lemon (2 Tbsp)

½ tsp kosher salt

⅛ tsp coarsely ground black pepper

1. Preheat oven to 400°F. Spray a baking pan with nonstick cooking spray.

2. Place salmon fillets into prepared baking pan. Season with salt, onion powder, garlic powder, and paprika. Rest seasoned fish for 10 minutes for flavors to meld.

3. **Prepare the marinade:** In a small bowl, whisk together oil, garlic, parsley, lemon zest, lemon juice, salt, and pepper.

4. Brush marinade generously over salmon. Rest fish for 5-10 minutes.

5. Bake for 15-17 minutes. Remove from oven; baste with marinade.

---Tip---

To avoid cross contamination, wash and dry the basting brush that touched raw fish before using the brush again on the cooked fish.

LEMON-MAPLE GLAZED SIDE OF SALMON

Pareve YIELDS *6-8 servings*

This superstar recipe made writing this cookbook worth the effort. This dish will not be retired from your repertoire. One bite and I know you will agree.

- **1** (2-3-lb) side salmon
- sea salt, to taste
- paprika, to taste
- onion powder, to taste
- garlic powder, to taste

Lemon-Maple Glaze

- **¼ cup** pure maple syrup
- **2 Tbsp** apricot jam
- **2 Tbsp** lemon juice
- **1 Tbsp** ketchup
- **3 cloves** garlic, crushed
- **1 Tbsp** fresh dill, chopped, *or* **1½ tsp** dried dill
- **½ tsp** kosher salt
- **¼ tsp** coarsely ground black pepper
- dill fronds, for garnish, optional

1. **Prepare the lemon maple glaze:** In a small bowl, whisk together all glaze ingredients until relatively smooth. Set aside.

2. **Prepare the salmon:** Preheat oven to 400°F. Line a baking sheet with parchment paper; spray with nonstick cooking spray.

3. Place side of salmon, skin-side down, onto prepared baking sheet. Dab salmon with a dry paper towel. Season to taste with listed spices or use your favorite seafood seasoning. Brush a generous amount of glaze onto fish. Allow to rest for 10 minutes.

4. Bake, uncovered, on the middle rack for 10 minutes. Remove baking sheet from oven; baste fish with a generous brushing of glaze. Return pan to oven. Repeat basting every 10 minutes for a total baking time of 30-35 minutes. Remove from the oven and baste one final time (see Tip).

5. Serve warm or at room temperature. Garnish with dill, if desired.

Variation
This recipe can be made using salmon fillets; bake for 15-17 minutes.

Tip
To avoid cross contamination, wash and dry the basting brush that touched raw fish before using the brush again on the cooked fish.

Poultry

CRANBBQ CHICKEN BAKE

Meat YIELDS *8 servings*

Simple, comforting, and delicious, this one-pan meal is just the ticket when you're looking for an easy and healthy weeknight meal.

2 medium	red or Yukon Gold potatoes, sliced into ¼-inch-thick rounds
1 large	sweet potato, sliced into ¼-inch-thick rounds
2 Tbsp	olive oil
½ tsp	kosher salt
¼ tsp	coarsely ground black pepper
8	chicken bottoms
•	onion powder, to taste
•	garlic powder, to taste
•	kosher salt, to taste
•	paprika, to taste

CranBBQ Glaze

½ cup	BBQ sauce
½ cup	jellied cranberry sauce
1 Tbsp	balsamic vinegar
⅛ tsp	ground ginger

1. Preheat oven to 375°F.

2. In a roasting pan, large enough to hold the chicken in a single layer, toss sliced potatoes with olive oil, salt, and pepper.

3. Place chicken over potatoes. Season lightly with spices. Seal pan tightly with foil. Bake, covered, for 45 minutes.

4. **Meanwhile, prepare the cranBBQ glaze:** In a cup or small bowl, whisk together glaze ingredients.

5. Remove pan from oven. Spread glaze over chicken. Return pan to oven; bake 45 minutes, uncovered, until tender.

— Tip —

This recipe can be easily halved or doubled!

— Note —

You can also use chicken bottoms that were separated into drumsticks and thighs, as pictured.

HONEY-MUSTARD DRUMSTICKS

Meat   YIELDS *4-5 servings*

With a 5-ingredient glaze and no marinating required, these chicken drumsticks are golden, sticky, and finger-lickin' good.

8-10 chicken drumsticks

• onion powder, to taste

• garlic powder, to taste

• kosher salt, to taste

• black pepper, to taste

• paprika, to taste

Honey-Mustard Glaze

⅓ cup honey

¼ cup spicy brown mustard or mustard of choice

3 cloves garlic, crushed

3 Tbsp olive oil

2 Tbsp lemon juice

1. Preheat oven to 350°F.

2. Place drumsticks into a 9x13-inch baking pan. Lightly season with spices. Bake, covered, for 30 minutes on center rack.

3. **Meanwhile, prepare the honey-mustard glaze:** In a cup or small bowl, whisk together glaze ingredients.

4. Remove pan from oven. Pour accumulated liquid into a small bowl. (Allow liquid to cool; discard.)

5. Pour glaze over drumsticks. Bake, uncovered, 30-40 minutes, until tender.

EILEEN'S
SWEET AND TANGY CHICKEN

Meat YIELDS *8 servings*

Everything about my friend Eileen a"h exuded life. Although it has been a number of years since her untimely passing, each time I make this chicken on the bone I think of Eileen and her glorious legacy. Thank you, Rochie, for sharing her spectacular recipe with me.

8 chicken bottoms

• sea salt, to taste

• garlic powder, to taste

• onion powder, to taste

• paprika, to taste

½ cup mayonnaise

½ cup cornflake crumbs

Sweet and Tangy Sauce

1 cup duck sauce

½ cup honey

3 Tbsp yellow mustard

3 Tbsp low sodium soy sauce

1. Preheat oven to 350°F. Grease a roasting pan.

2. Place chicken into prepared pan. Season chicken lightly with spices. Spread mayonnaise over chicken. Sprinkle with cornflake crumbs to evenly cover.

3. Cover; bake on center rack for 1 hour 20 minutes.

4. **Meanwhile, prepare the sweet and tangy sauce:** In a small bowl, combine sauce ingredients.

5. Remove pan from oven. Pour accumulated liquid into a small bowl. (Allow liquid to cool; discard.)

6. Pour sauce over chicken. Return pan to oven. Bake, uncovered, for 20-30 minutes, until tender.

— Note —

You can also use chicken bottoms that were separated into drumsticks and thighs, as pictured.

HOT HONEY WINGS

Meat   YIELDS *4-6 servings*

These aren't just any hot wings. These wings are coated in a flavorful rub and then smothered in a perfect combination of honey and heat ... AKA the best wings ever! These hot wings will fly off the plate — literally!

2 lb	chicken wings, patted dry
1 Tbsp	chili powder
1 Tbsp	kosher salt
⅛ tsp	cayenne pepper, optional

Hot Honey Sauce

•	juice of 1 lime
½ cup	honey
1-2 Tbsp	sriracha *or* hot sauce
1 Tbsp	ketchup
¼-½ tsp	crushed red pepper flakes
4 cloves	garlic, coarsely chopped

Garnish

2-3	jalapeños, thinly sliced
1	lime, cut into wedges

1. In a large bowl, combine chili powder, salt, and cayenne pepper, if using. Add wings; toss and rub with spice mixture. Allow to rest for 15 minutes or refrigerate for up to 1 day.

2. Preheat oven to 375°F. Line a baking sheet with foil.

3. Arrange wings on prepared baking sheet. Bake 40 minutes on center rack.

4. **Prepare the hot honey sauce:** In a large bowl, combine lime juice, honey, sriracha, ketchup, red pepper flakes, and garlic. Add chicken wings; toss to coat. Return wings to baking sheet. Discard any remaining sauce.

5. Preheat oven to broil.

6. Broil wings until golden brown, 5-8 minutes. Alternatively, grill wings until golden.

7. Transfer wings to serving platter. Garnish with sliced jalapeños and lime wedges.

SWEET HEAT CHICKEN SUBS

Meat YIELDS *4-6 servings*

This is one of our all-time favorite weeknight dinners. It's super quick to prepare, with a sweet heat kick. One bite of this jalapeño-and-honey chicken nestled in a sub or a taco shell, and you'll agree this recipe is off the charts.

2 lb	ground chicken, preferably dark meat
2 Tbsp	olive oil
1 large	onion, diced (see Note)
1	jalapeño, finely diced
½ cup	honey
2-3 Tbsp	lime juice
2 Tbsp	rice vinegar
2 Tbsp	ketchup
2 Tbsp	low sodium soy sauce
2 Tbsp	dried parsley flakes
3 cloves	garlic, crushed
¼-½ tsp	hot sauce
¼ tsp	ground ginger
¼ tsp	kosher salt
¼ tsp	cayenne pepper
2-3	baguettes, cut in half
•	sweet chili sauce
•	lettuce, optional
•	tomatoes, optional

1. In a large skillet, heat olive oil over medium heat. Add onion; sauté for 15 minutes, until lightly golden. Add jalapeño; sauté an additional 3 minutes.

2. Add honey, lime juice, rice vinegar, ketchup, soy sauce, parsley, garlic, hot sauce, ginger, salt, and cayenne pepper. Raise heat; bring mixture to a rolling boil.

3. Reduce heat to medium. Add ground chicken. Cook for about 10 minutes, stirring to break up any chunks, until cooked through. Remove from heat.

4. **Assemble subs:** Spread sweet chili sauce on inside surface of baguette. Top with a serving of ground chicken. Add lettuce and tomatoes, if desired.

---Variation---

Serve chicken over rice or pasta or in a lettuce cup, if desired.

---Note---

Short on time? Substitute 3 cubes frozen sautéed onions for the sautéed onion.

SESAME CHICKEN

Meat   YIELDS *6 servings*

This sesame chicken is seriously so delectable, you'll be tempted to toss those take-out menus. These crispy chicken pieces coated in a sweet and savory honey sesame sauce are perfectly delicious. I think this homemade version is even better than what I've had at many restaurants. My kids most definitely agree.

1½ lb	dark chicken cutlets
¼ cup	nondairy milk
3 cloves	garlic, crushed
⅛ tsp	crushed red pepper flakes
•	canola oil, for frying
2 tsp	sesame oil
•	chopped chives, for garnish

Batter

½ cup	cornstarch
½ cup	flour
½ cup	cold seltzer
2	egg whites

Sesame Sauce

¼ cup	low sodium soy sauce
¼ cup	rice vinegar
¼ cup	dark brown sugar
¼ cup	honey
¼ cup	ketchup
1 Tbsp	cornstarch
⅓ cup	water
1 tsp	garlic powder
1 Tbsp	black and white sesame seeds + more for garnish

1. In a large resealable bag, combine nondairy milk, garlic, and red pepper flakes. Add chicken tenders. Coat chicken tenders; marinate and soften for 15-20 minutes.

2. In a large bowl, combine and whisk together batter ingredients. Add marinated chicken tenders. Discard remaining marinade. Mix to completely coat with batter.

3. Heat 3 inches oil in a 2-3-quart saucepan over medium heat. Add a few pieces of chicken at a time, taking care not to crowd the pan. Fry for 2 minutes, until lightly golden. Turn chicken; fry until lightly golden. Transfer fried chicken to a paper towel-lined cooling rack or pan. Repeat until all chicken is fried.

4. **Prepare the sesame sauce:** In a small bowl, whisk together sauce ingredients until smooth. Set aside.

5. Heat sesame oil in a large skillet or wok over medium heat. Add sesame sauce. Bring to a boil; cook until thickened, whisking occasionally. Reduce heat to medium-low. Add fried chicken; toss to coat with sauce.

6. Before serving, sprinkle with additional sesame seeds and chopped chives.

— Note
White chicken cutlets also work here, but dark cutlets are a bit juicier.

PESTO CHICKEN STIR FRY

Meat YIELDS *4 servings*

This easy pesto chicken stir fry is quite versatile and can be served with any pasta, potato, or rice side (as pictured). It is out-of-this-world good and will appeal even to those who aren't usually pesto fans.

5 Tbsp	prepared pesto, divided (page 100)
1 lb	thin chicken cutlets, cut into narrow strips
1 medium/ large	red onion, thinly sliced
2 cloves	garlic, crushed
3 Tbsp	sweet chili sauce
2 Tbsp	low sodium soy sauce
1 tsp	dried basil
1 tsp	lime juice

1. In a medium bowl, combine 3 tablespoons pesto with chicken slivers. Toss to coat well. Set aside to marinate for at least 10 minutes or overnight in the refrigerator.

2. In a large skillet, over medium-high heat, heat remaining 2 tablespoons pesto. Add onion and garlic. Cook, stirring, for 3-5 minutes, until onions have softened. Add marinated chicken; cook, stirring occasionally, for 5-7 minutes, until the chicken is cooked through.

3. Stir in remaining ingredients. Bring mixture to a boil. Remove from heat.

SWEET AND SOUR STUFFED CAPONS

Meat   YIELDS *8-10 servings*

Easy to prepare, yet elegant enough for guests or special occasions. Shout out to Tante Edie for this timeless classic stuffing.

8-10 capons (boneless thighs)
• onion powder, to taste
• garlic powder, to taste
• kosher salt, to taste
• black pepper, to taste
• paprika, to taste

Stuffing

1 large onion, diced
6 oz pastrami, sliced and diced, optional
3 Tbsp olive oil
1 sleeve snackers crackers, crushed
• onion powder, to taste
• garlic powder, to taste
• kosher salt, to taste
• black pepper, to taste
• paprika, to taste
1 egg
¼ cup nondairy milk

Sweet and Sour Glaze

¼ cup chili sauce
2 Tbsp olive oil
2 Tbsp dark brown sugar
2 Tbsp lemon juice
2 Tbsp mirin
2 cloves garlic, crushed

1. Preheat oven to 350°F. Prepare an oven-to-table cookware or baking dish large enough to hold the capons in a single layer.

2. **Prepare the stuffing:** In a skillet, over medium-high heat, sauté onions and pastrami (if using) in olive oil until lightly golden, about 15 minutes, stirring occasionally.

3. Place crushed crackers into a small bowl. Season with spices. Add egg and nondairy milk. Add onion-pastrami mixture. Mix to combine.

4. Add 1 heaping tablespoon of stuffing onto the center of each capon. Fold all the sides around stuffing; place capons into prepared baking dish. The tighter they are packed, the nicer the baked shape will be.

5. Sprinkle spices over filled capons. Cover pan with foil; bake on the center rack for 1 hour.

6. **Meanwhile, prepare the sweet and sour glaze:** Combine glaze ingredients in a cup or bowl.

7. Remove capons from oven. Pour accumulated liquid into a small bowl. (Allow liquid to cool; discard.)

8. Pour glaze evenly over capons. Return to oven and bake 1 hour, covered, basting periodically.

CRISPY BAKED LEMON-HERB CHICKEN

Meat   YIELDS *6 servings*

We eat lots of chicken during the week, so I am always thinking of ways to make it just a bit different. When I made this ultra-crispy on the outside, incredibly juicy on the inside, with just the right lemony-flavored chicken, it quickly became a dinner staple.

6	chicken cutlets, not thinly sliced, each cut into 4 fingers
½ cup	mayonnaise
1 Tbsp	Dijon mustard
2 Tbsp	lemon juice
•	zest of 1 lemon
¾ cup	panko crumbs
1 Tbsp	dried parsley
½ tsp	dried dill

Creamy Lemon Aioli

¼ cup	mayonnaise
1 clove	garlic, crushed
1 Tbsp	lemon juice
2 tsp	olive oil
1½ tsp	lemon zest

1. Preheat oven to 350°F. Line a baking sheet with parchment paper.

2. **Prepare the chicken:** In a small bowl, combine mayonnaise, mustard, lemon juice, and lemon zest. In a second bowl, combine panko and dried herbs.

3. Dredge chicken in mayonnaise mixture and then in the panko mixture. Place chicken on prepared baking sheet. Bake for 30 minutes.

4. **Meanwhile, prepare the creamy lemon aioli:** In a small bowl, whisk together aioli ingredients. Set aside.

5. Serve chicken with creamy lemon aioli.

SIMPLE
SUPPER

BEST-DRESSED CHICKEN CUTLETS

Meat YIELDS *4-6 servings*

I challenged myself to come up with a chicken recipe to rival the ever-popular Marinated Grilled Chicken in "Simply Gourmet." I can humbly say, mission accomplished.

4-6 chicken cutlets

Marinade

¼ cup	olive oil
2 cloves	garlic, crushed
2 Tbsp	dark brown sugar
2 Tbsp	ketchup
1½ Tbsp	lemon juice
1½ Tbsp	low sodium soy sauce
1 tsp	Dijon mustard
½ tsp	fish-free Worcestershire sauce
½ tsp	sea salt
¼ tsp	coarsely ground black pepper

1. Combine marinade ingredients in a large resealable bag. Add chicken; mix well to completely coat.

2. Marinate for at least 30 minutes, or, ideally, for 4-5 hours in the refrigerator.

3. Heat a grill pan or skillet. Remove chicken from marinade. Grill 3-5 minutes on each side, depending on thickness. Discard remaining marinade.

SIMPLE SUPPER

PERFECT PARGIOT WITH CHIMICHURRI SAUCE

Meat YIELDS *6-8 servings*

Humble boneless chicken thighs, also known as pargiot, can be transformed into the most delicious, juicy dish with this marinade. The tangy chimichurri is the best accompaniment, and brings the pargiot over the top.

6-8	skinless, boneless chicken thighs
¼ cup	balsamic vinegar
¼ cup	Italian dressing
1 Tbsp	Dijon mustard
2 Tbsp	honey
1 tsp	chili powder
•	lemon slices, for garnish, optional

Chimichurri Sauce

¼ cup	red wine vinegar
4 cloves	garlic
½ small	red onion
2 cups	fresh parsley leaves
1	scallion (white and light green parts only)
1	jalapeño pepper, halved and seeded
1 tsp	kosher salt
1 tsp	dried oregano
¼-½ tsp	coarsely ground black pepper
½ cup	olive oil

1. **Prepare the chimichurri sauce:** Place all sauce ingredients into food processor fitted with the S-blade. Pulse until evenly blended. To release all its flavors, allow chimichurri to rest for at least 10 minutes before using. If time allows, 2 hours is optimum. Chimichurri will remain fresh in an airtight container in the refrigerator for 2 days.

2. In a large resealable bag, combine balsamic vinegar, Italian dressing, mustard, honey, and chili powder. Add chicken to bag; marinate at room temperature for at least 30 minutes.

3. Preheat grill or grill pan on medium-high heat.

4. Remove chicken from marinade. Remove pan from heat; coat grill/grill pan with cooking spray. Return pan to heat. Grill chicken for 7-8 minutes per side, until cooked through. Discard remaining marinade. Alternatively, chicken can be baked with its marinade at 400°F for 25-30 minutes, until baked through.

5. Remove to a platter. Garnish with lemon slices, if desired; serve with chimichurri sauce.

STICKY PASTRAMI MUSHROOM CHICKEN

Meat YIELDS *4-6 servings*

On the lookout for a new supper idea? Look no further. While this marinated chicken is in the oven, a few simple pantry ingredients create the wonderful sauce that completes the dish. The chicken is then coated in the sweet and sticky sauce and baked to perfection.

8	thin chicken cutlets
¼ cup	Italian dressing
¼ cup	teriyaki sauce

Sweet 'N Pungent Sauce

3 Tbsp	olive oil
1 large	onion, diced
4 cloves	garlic, crushed
6 oz	pastrami, sliced thinly and diced
10 oz	mushrooms, sliced ½-inch-thick
10 oz	apricot jam
½ cup	sweet chili sauce
3 Tbsp	dark brown sugar
1 tsp	kosher salt
½ tsp	coarsely ground black pepper

1. Preheat oven to 400°F. Line a baking sheet with parchment paper; coat with cooking spray.

2. Combine Italian dressing and teriyaki sauce in a large resealable bag. Add chicken; marinate for 30 minutes.

3. Place cutlets onto prepared baking sheet. Discard remaining marinade. Bake, uncovered, for 7 minutes. Turn cutlets; bake for an additional 7 minutes.

4. **Meanwhile prepare the sweet 'n pungent sauce:** Heat olive oil in a large skillet over medium-high heat. Add onion; sauté until slightly golden, 6-8 minutes. Add garlic, stirring for 30 seconds, until fragrant. Add mushrooms and pastrami; sauté until softened.

5. Stir in jam, sweet chili sauce, brown sugar, salt, and pepper. Simmer until bubbly.

6. Remove chicken from oven. Spoon onion-mushroom mixture over cutlets. Return to oven; bake, covered, for 7 minutes.

7. Serve warm.

CHICKEN WITH PESTO, SHALLOT, AND WHITE WINE SAUCE

Meat   YIELDS *6-8 servings*

With its gourmet sauce, this rich and savory dish is bursting with flavor. In under 30 minutes, with one pan and just a few ingredients, this amazing dinner can be on your table.

8-10	extra thinly sliced chicken cutlets
¼ cup	prepared pesto (page 100)
⅓ cup	cornstarch
½ tsp	sea salt
¼ tsp	coarsely ground black pepper
¼ cup	olive oil

Pesto, Shallot, and White Wine Sauce

2 Tbsp	olive oil
½ cup	sliced shallots
½ cup	white wine (dry or semi-sweet, depending on preference)
½ cup	chicken broth
½ cup	prepared pesto (page 100)

1. Marinate chicken in pesto for 15-30 minutes.

2. Place cornstarch on a plate. Stir in salt and pepper. Dredge chicken cutlets in cornstarch.

3. Heat olive oil in a large skillet over medium-high heat. Pan-sear each cutlet for 1 minute on each side, until cooked through. Discard remaining marinade. Transfer chicken to a serving tray. After all cutlets are fried, wipe out the pan.

4. **Prepare the pesto, shallot, and white wine sauce:** In the same pan, sauté shallots in olive oil until soft and translucent, 5-8 minutes. Add wine, broth, and prepared pesto. Simmer for 5 minutes.

5. Pour sauce over cutlets. Serve warm.

LEMON-GLAZED DUCK BREAST

Meat   YIELDS *4 servings*

Elevated presentation and speedy preparation. Foodies, this one is definitely for you.

4 boneless duck breasts

• kosher salt, to taste

• black pepper, to taste

Lemon Simple Syrup and Candied Lemons

1 cup sugar

¾ cup water

• juice of 1 small lemon

1 small lemon, thinly sliced

Lemon Glaze

4 Tbsp lemon simple syrup

4 Tbsp semi-sweet white wine

2 tsp cornstarch

1. Preheat oven to 400°F. Set out a large frying pan.

2. Score duck breasts (lightly slice into the skin without cutting through to the meat). Season lightly with salt and pepper.

3. Lay duck breasts skin-side down in prepared pan over medium-high heat. This will render the fat between the skin and the meat. Sear the duck for 6 minutes. Turn duck; sear second side for 1-2 minutes.

4. Transfer duck breasts to a 9x13-inch baking pan. Bake for 7-10 minutes for medium rare.

5. **Prepare the lemon simple syrup and candied lemons:** In a frying pan, over medium heat, combine sugar, water, and lemon juice. Bring to a boil, stirring until sugar has dissolved. Lower heat to a simmer. Add lemon slices in a single layer; cook for about 15 minutes. Turn slices occasionally. Using tongs, transfer lemon slices onto parchment paper to cool. Set aside, reserving the lemon simple syrup for the duck glaze.

6. **Prepare the lemon glaze:** In a small saucepan over medium-low heat, combine glaze ingredients. Stir over heat until slightly thickened.

7. **To serve:** Place duck on a serving platter. Drizzle with lemon glaze. Top with candied lemons.

—Note

The lemon simple syrup and candied lemons can be prepared 2-3 days in advance, but the duck is best when served fresh.

Meat

GARLICKY MEATBALLS

Meat   **YIELDS** *6 servings*

Serve these delicious meatballs with your favorite pasta and make your weeknight dinner a memorable one.

2 lb	ground beef
½ cup	seasoned breadcrumbs
1	egg
¼ cup	nondairy milk
2 cloves	garlic, crushed
½ tsp	onion powder
½ tsp	garlic powder

Garlicky Sauce

1 (14-oz) can	jellied cranberry sauce
24 oz	marinara sauce
3 Tbsp	lemon juice
3 cloves	garlic, crushed
1 tsp	dried oregano
1 tsp	dried basil
½ tsp	coarsely ground black pepper
¼ tsp	sea salt

1. **Prepare the garlicky sauce:** In a 3-quart pot, over medium heat, melt cranberry sauce, mashing with a fork to break it up. Add marinara sauce and lemon juice. Stir to combine. Bring to a boil. Stir in remaining sauce ingredients. Reduce heat to a medium simmer.

2. **Prepare the meatballs:** Combine ground beef with remaining meatball ingredients. Shape into 2-inch balls; slip into simmering sauce. Cover; bring to a boil. Reduce heat to medium-low; cook for 30-40 minutes.

— Note

Serve meatballs and sauce over a bed of rice, potatoes, or spaghetti.

SAVORY BEEF CROSTATA

Meat **YIELDS** *6 servings*

This savory, homey tart, with its hand-rolled flakey dough, is filled with meaty goodness.

Crust

¾ cup	flour
½ cup	whole wheat flour
¼ tsp	kosher salt
½ tsp	dried basil
½ tsp	dried oregano
½ cup	chilled margarine (1 stick), diced
3 Tbsp	ice water
2-3 Tbsp	nondairy milk, for brushing

Beef Filling

1 Tbsp	olive oil
1 small	onion, diced
2 cloves	garlic, crushed
3½ oz	shiitake mushrooms, sliced
1	red pepper, cut into 1-inch matchsticks
⅓ cup	nondairy milk
¼ cup	dry white wine
1 tsp	Dijon mustard
1 tsp	kosher salt
½ tsp	dried basil
½ tsp	dried oregano
¼ tsp	coarsely ground black pepper
1 lb	ground beef

Garlic-Basil Dressing

¼ cup	mayonnaise
1 Tbsp	vinegar
1 tsp	dried basil
2 tsp	silan or honey
½ tsp	Dijon mustard
1 clove	garlic, crushed

1. **Prepare the crust:** In a medium bowl, mix together flours, salt, basil, and oregano. Add margarine. Cut mixture with a pastry cutter or crumble by hand until mixture reaches a crumbly consistency. Sprinkle ice water over the mixture; knead until a dough forms. Roll into a ball, wrap in plastic wrap, and refrigerate for 1 hour.

2. **Meanwhile, prepare the beef filling:** In a large frying pan, heat olive oil. Add onion and garlic; sauté over medium heat until onion is translucent, about 3 minutes. Add mushrooms and pepper; cook an additional 2 minutes. Stir in nondairy milk, wine, mustard, and spices. Stir to combine. Add ground beef. With a large spoon, break up the meat; cook until beef separates, becomes crumbly, and is no longer pink. Set aside.

3. **Prepare the garlic-basil dressing:** In a small bowl, thoroughly combine dressing ingredients. Set aside.

4. Preheat oven to 350°F. Set out a baking sheet.

5. **Assemble the crostata:** Between 2 pieces of parchment paper, roll out dough into a 14-inch circle about ¼-inch-thick. (It's important to roll your dough out thinly so it doesn't open like a flower during the baking process.) Remove top parchment paper. Transfer crostata with the parchment paper to prepared baking sheet.

6. Spread a thin layer of garlic-basil dressing onto the center of the circle, leaving a 2-inch border. (Reserve remaining dressing for serving.) Pile meat mixture onto dressing until the border of the dressing. Fold edges of dough up and over meat mixture in a series of pleats. Brush edges liberally with nondairy milk.

7. Bake 25-30 minutes until crust is golden brown. Drizzle crostata with remaining dressing or serve dressing alongside as a dipping sauce. Serve warm.

BBQ BEEF
WITH ORECCHIETTE

 Meat **YIELDS** *6 servings*

This is truly the VERY BEST homemade Sloppy Joe EVER! It is quick, economical, and reminiscent of your childhood favorite, only better.

2 lb	ground beef
1 Tbsp	olive oil
1 medium	onion, diced
4 cloves	garlic, crushed
1 (8-oz) can	tomato sauce
2 Tbsp	dark brown sugar, packed
1 Tbsp	Dijon mustard
1½-2 tsp	chili powder
1 tsp	fish-free Worcestershire sauce
3 Tbsp	apple cider vinegar
3 Tbsp	BBQ sauce
12 oz	orecchiette pasta *or* pasta of choice, prepared according to package directions

1. In a large skillet, over medium heat, heat olive oil. Add onion; sauté for 10 minutes, stirring occasionally. Add crushed garlic; continue to sauté for 3 minutes, stirring occasionally.

2. Add tomato sauce, brown sugar, mustard, chili powder, Worcestershire sauce, vinegar, and BBQ sauce. Bring to a boil. Add ground beef, breaking it into small pieces. Stir until beef separates, becomes crumbly, and is completely incorporated into the sauce.

3. Press mixture down to ensure all the meat is cooking through. Cook for a few minutes; stir. Repeat every few minutes for 15-20 minutes, until beef is completely cooked.

4. Toss beef with prepared pasta.

SIMPLE SUPPER

SAUCY BURGERS

Meat **YIELDS** *6-8 servings*

Alone or on a bun, these burgers are bursting with so much flavor, there's no need for any condiments.

2 lb	ground beef
3 Tbsp	breadcrumbs
1	egg
2 Tbsp	ketchup
2 Tbsp	yellow mustard
1 Tbsp	BBQ sauce
½ tsp	onion powder
½ tsp	garlic powder
½ tsp	sea salt
3 Tbsp	olive oil, for frying

Sauce

1 cup	diced onion (about 1 large onion)
1 cup	sliced mushrooms (white or baby bella)
¾ tsp	sea salt, divided
¼ tsp	coarsely ground black pepper, divided
1 small	yellow pepper, diced
1 (16-oz) can	tomato sauce
½ cup	water
2 Tbsp	balsamic vinegar *or* fish-free Worcestershire sauce

1. In a large bowl, combine ground beef, breadcrumbs, egg, ketchup, mustard, BBQ sauce, onion powder, garlic powder, and salt. Mix well.

2. In a large skillet, over medium-high heat, heat oil.

3. Shape meat into about 8 patties. Brown patties on both sides, 3 minutes per side; remove to a serving tray.

4. **Prepare the sauce:** Add diced onion to oil remaining in the skillet (add more oil if necessary). Sauté onion, stirring occasionally, until lightly golden, 7-8 minutes. Add mushrooms; season with some of the salt and pepper. Cook, stirring occasionally, until any moisture released by mushrooms has evaporated, 4-6 minutes.

5. Add yellow pepper; season again with salt and pepper. Stir until yellow pepper has softened, about 2 minutes. Add tomato sauce, water, and balsamic vinegar. Bring to a boil. Reduce heat to a simmer.

6. Gently place burgers into sauce; simmer, uncovered, for 15-20 minutes, basting occasionally.

―Serving Suggestion―――――――――
Serve saucy burgers in a burger bun, topped with sauce, lettuce, and tomato.

Meat

BEEF STEW

Pure comfort food, this classic homestyle beef stew is simmered in broth with potatoes, onions, and carrots until it is melt-in-your-mouth tender. If you are feeding a crowd, this doubles beautifully.

Meat   **YIELDS** *4-6 servings*

2 Tbsp	olive oil
1½ lb	stew meat, cubed
•	sea salt, to taste
•	black pepper, to taste
2 large	onions, sliced
2 ribs	celery, sliced
1 Tbsp	dried parsley flakes
1 tsp	dried oregano
1 tsp	dried basil
1 tsp	sea salt
½ tsp	onion powder
½ tsp	garlic powder
½-¾ tsp	coarsely ground black pepper
1 (15-oz) can	tomato sauce
1 (15-oz) can	stewed tomatoes
2 Tbsp	tomato paste
2 Tbsp	red wine vinegar
3 cloves	garlic, crushed
¾ cup	dry red wine
¾ cup	beef broth *or* **¾ cup** water + **¾ tsp** beef broth powder
1 lb	baby potatoes, halved
•	dill, for garnish, optional

1. Season meat with salt and pepper.

2. In a large Dutch oven or ovenproof pot over medium-high heat, heat oil. Add onions and meat. Sear meat on all sides. Add celery and spices. Stir well. Add tomato sauce, stewed tomatoes, tomato paste, vinegar, garlic, wine, and beef broth. Stir well. Cover stew; cook over low heat for 20 minutes.

3. Meanwhile, preheat oven to 325°F.

4. Add potatoes to stew; stir well. Transfer pot to oven. Bake, covered, for 2 hours. Garnish with dill, if desired.

Tip

If you do not have an ovenproof pot, transfer stew to a 9x13-inch baking pan before placing into oven.

BEEF AND BROCCOLI RAMEN BOWL

Meat   **YIELDS** *4 servings*

Fast and healthy, made in 15 minutes from start to finish. Less expensive, and healthier than takeout, too.

½ cup	low sodium soy sauce
1½ Tbsp	cornstarch
6 Tbsp	rice vinegar
4 Tbsp	hoisin sauce
4 Tbsp	dark brown sugar
½ tsp	ground ginger
5 tsp	sesame oil, divided
¼ tsp	crushed red pepper flakes
2 cups	water
2 (3-oz) packages	ramen noodles
2 Tbsp	canola oil, divided
1 lb	New York-style strip steak or rib steak, sliced thinly across the grain
4 cloves	garlic, crushed
16 oz	broccoli florets
1 Tbsp	toasted sesame seeds
4	scallions, sliced

1. In a small bowl, combine soy sauce and cornstarch to create a slurry. Add rice vinegar, hoisin sauce, brown sugar, ginger, 4 teaspoons sesame oil, and red pepper flakes. Stir until thoroughly combined. Set aside.

2. In a 2-quart saucepan, bring water to a boil. Add ramen noodles with 1 spice packet. Boil for 3 minutes. Remove from heat; drain. Add remaining teaspoon sesame oil. Toss to combine.

3. In a large skillet over medium heat, heat 1 tablespoon oil. Add beef strips and crushed garlic. Stir fry for 3 minutes. Use a slotted spoon to transfer beef to a bowl.

4. Add remaining tablespoon oil to the skillet. Add broccoli; stir fry for 2 minutes. Add soy sauce mixture to the skillet; add beef. Stir fry until sauce thickens. Add prepared ramen noodles to the skillet. Toss to combine.

5. Transfer to a serving bowl or individual bowls. Toss with sesame seeds and scallions.

BABY LAMB CHOPS WITH ROASTED GARLIC VINAIGRETTE

Meat   **YIELDS** *2-3 servings*

You might be wondering: Vinaigrette on a lamb chop? My answer is a resounding, "Absolutely yes!" With its fragrant roasted garlic flavor, this dressing definitely delivers the WOW factor.

6 baby lamb chops

• kosher salt, to taste

• black pepper, to taste

1 Tbsp honey

Roasted Garlic Vinaigrette

1 head garlic

1 Tbsp olive oil

½ tsp kosher salt, divided

¼ tsp coarsely ground black pepper, divided

¼ cup pine nuts

1-1½ Tbsp lemon juice

½ cup olive oil

¼ cup fresh parsley, chopped, *or* **1½ Tbsp** dried parsley flakes

1. **Prepare the roasted garlic vinaigrette:** Preheat oven to 350°F.

2. Slice off the top of the garlic head, exposing the cloves. Place garlic head on a small piece of foil. Drizzle with olive oil; sprinkle with ¼ teaspoon salt and ⅛ teaspoon pepper. Wrap foil around the head. Place wrapped garlic into a muffin tin holder or on a baking sheet. Bake 30-40 minutes, until garlic is soft. Remove from oven; allow to cool.

3. While garlic is roasting, place pine nuts into a baking pan; toast for 5-7 minutes in the oven. Remove from oven; allow to cool.

4. Push garlic cloves out of the head into a small bowl by pushing upward from the bottom. Add lemon juice and olive oil. Puree with an immersion blender. Stir in parsley, pine nuts, and remaining ¼ teaspoon salt and ⅛ teaspoon pepper.

5. Season lamb chops with salt and pepper. Score lamb chops about ⅛-inch-deep, taking care not to cut too deep.

6. Preheat a cast iron or stainless-steel grill pan until smoking, over medium-high heat. Off the heat, grease with olive oil or cooking spray.

7. Sear or grill lamb chops for 3-4 minutes. Drizzle each chop with a little honey before turning each chop over; grill on second side for 3-4 minutes.

8. Serve vinaigrette alongside lamb chops.

CHILI-LIME HANGER STEAK

Meat **YIELDS** *4 servings*

The secret to this juicy, incredible steak is the amazing marinade. It yields such full, incredible taste and packs plenty of zesty flavor into every tender bite.

1½-2 lb hanger steak

Chili-Lime Marinade

2 Tbsp	white wine vinegar
2 Tbsp	lime juice
4 cloves	garlic, crushed
2 Tbsp	low sodium soy sauce
2 Tbsp	dark brown sugar
2 Tbsp	honey
2 tsp	smoked paprika
2 tsp	chili powder
1 tsp	kosher salt
1 tsp	coarsely ground black pepper

1. Place hanger steak into a large bowl; add water to cover. Soak for 20 minutes to remove saltiness; remove to a plate.

2. Meanwhile, combine marinade ingredients in a large bowl or resealable bag. Mix well until combined.

3. Add hanger steak to marinade, making sure meat is completely coated. Marinate at room temperature for 30 minutes. Alternatively, marinate in the fridge for up to 8 hours.

4. Preheat grill or oven to high broil.

5. Remove meat from marinade; discard any remaining marinade. Broil or grill meat for 4 minutes on each side. Let meat rest for 5-10 minutes. Slice into thin slices diagonally across the grain.

—Variation

Hanger steak can be substituted with skirt steak or oyster steak. For skirt steak, follow above directions. Oyster steak does not need to soak and should be seared for 1-2 minutes per side and then baked in a 350°F oven for 5-10 minutes.

HERB-MARINATED LONDON BROIL

Meat   **YIELDS** *6 servings*

For many years I had my go-to London broil recipe. Since developing this new version, I haven't looked back. Try it and you'll agree.

1 (2-lb)   London broil

• parsley, for garnish, optional

Marinade

¼ cup   olive oil

2 Tbsp   low sodium soy sauce

3 Tbsp   lemon juice

2 Tbsp   fish-free Worcestershire sauce

1 Tbsp   dried parsley flakes

1 tsp   dried basil

1 tsp   dried oregano

½ tsp   coarsely ground black pepper

1. Combine marinade ingredients in a large resealable bag. Add London broil; marinate for 30 minutes.

2. Preheat oven to high broil. Transfer meat and marinade to a 9x13-inch baking pan.

3. Broil for approximately 5 minutes on each side. Meat should read 125°F on a meat thermometer for medium rare.

4. Let meat rest for 10 minutes. Slice against the grain. Garnish with parsley, if desired.

VEAL POCKET WITH HONEY GLAZE

Meat **YIELDS** *6-10 servings*

The perfect balance of sweet and heat is infused into this veal by braising in a dry rub and later glazing with the hot honey. The depth of flavor appeals to those who like it hot and those who do not.

1 (3-5-lb) veal roast with pocket and bones

½ cup chicken stock *or* **½ cup** water + **½ tsp** consommé powder

½ cup white wine *or* **additional ½ cup** chicken stock

Dry Rub

2 Tbsp kosher salt

1 Tbsp coarsely ground black pepper

1 Tbsp onion powder

1 Tbsp garlic powder

1 Tbsp smoked paprika

1 Tbsp dried parsley flakes

Honey Glaze

½ cup honey

¼ cup rice vinegar (see Note)

1 Tbsp lime juice

¼ tsp ground ginger

⅛ tsp crushed red pepper flakes *or* **½-1 tsp** hot sauce

1. Preheat oven to 450°F. Set out a baking pan.

2. Pat veal dry; place into prepared pan.

3. **Prepare the dry rub:** In a small bowl, combine dry rub ingredients.

4. Spread rub over top and bottom of the veal, as well as inside the pocket. Pour chicken stock and white wine around the roast.

5. Bake, uncovered, for 20 minutes. Place a piece of parchment paper over roast; cover loosely with foil. (The paper prevents the foil from discoloring or warping.) Reduce heat to 325°F; bake for 3 hours.

6. **Prepare the honey glaze:** In a small saucepan over medium heat, combine glaze ingredients. Simmer for 5 minutes without stirring. Mixture will thicken and reduce.

7. Pour glaze over roast. Return roast to oven, uncovered. Roast for 30 minutes.

Optional

Double the glaze; pour on half the glaze in Step 5. Serve roast with remaining glaze on the side.

Note

If preferred, substitute apple cider vinegar or white wine vinegar for the rice vinegar.

MAPLE-GLAZED FRENCH ROAST

Meat **YIELDS** *6-10 servings*

Want a tender and flavorful French roast that's a sure bet? Well, here it is!

1 (3-5-lb)	French Roast
1 Tbsp	olive oil
1 Tbsp	kosher salt
1 tsp	coarsely ground black pepper

Maple Glaze

½ cup	pure maple syrup
3 Tbsp	vinegar *or* dry red wine
3 Tbsp	ketchup
3 Tbsp	yellow mustard
3 Tbsp	dried parsley flakes

1. Preheat oven to 450°F.

2. Place roast into a 9x13-inch baking pan. Drizzle olive oil over entire roast. Season with salt and pepper on both sides. Allow roast to rest for 10 minutes on the counter. Roast, uncovered, for 20 minutes.

3. **Meanwhile, prepare the maple glaze:** In a small bowl, combine all glaze ingredients. Mix well.

4. Remove roast from oven. Pour glaze over roast. Lower oven temperature to 325°F. Return pan to oven; roast for 35-45 minutes, basting every 15 minutes.

5. Let meat rest 15 minutes before slicing across the grain.

Note

To reheat, place sliced meat into pan sauce, cover, and warm in 250°F oven until ready to serve.

SALT-BAKED STANDING RIB ROAST

Meat   **YIELDS** *10-12 servings*

5-6-lb	bone-in standing rib roast
2 Tbsp	balsamic vinegar
6 cloves	garlic, crushed, *or* **6 cubes** frozen garlic
½ tsp	coarsely ground black pepper
4 cups	kosher salt
1 cup	water

Revealed beneath the salt crust, which is discarded after cooking, is the most magical, tender, juicy beef. This method is actually very easy and the results are beyond amazing.

1. Preheat oven to 450°F. Set out a roasting pan.

2. Brush balsamic vinegar over roast. Coat with garlic; sprinkle with pepper. Allow roast to stand at least 30 minutes to come to room temperature.

3. In a large bowl, combine salt and water. Mix until it becomes a snowy-like consistency.

4. Place a handful of salt into the roasting pan. Set roast on salt. Carefully pack remaining salt around the entire roast, working from the bottom up. (See photos on pages 201-202.) At this point, if desired, insert a meat thermometer into the roast and pack the salt around it. This will allow you to see the temperature of the roast as it cooks, as it will be difficult to insert a meat thermometer after the salt crust hardens.

5. Bake for 15 minutes.

6. Lower oven temperature to 325°F; continue to bake. Total cooking time will depend on the size of the roast; it should be about 15 minutes per pound. When the roast's internal temperature reaches 125°F-130°F for medium rare, or 145°F for medium, remove from oven. Let stand for 5 minutes.

7. Carefully remove hardened salt crust; brush any excess salt from roast. Transfer roast to a clean pan. Rest meat for 15 minutes before slicing.

Tip

Ask your butcher to separate the bone from the meat and then tie the two halves together. This will make slicing easier.

Meat

GLAZED CORNED BEEF

Meat   **YIELDS** *6-10 servings*

Brined beef brisket, AKA corned beef, is very versatile. Finished with this glaze, it can be served hot or at room temperature and is always equally delicious.

1 (3-5-lb)	pickled corned beef
1 Tbsp	vinegar
small handful	pickling spice
½ cup	apple juice

Glaze

12 oz	red currant jam (see Note)
2 Tbsp	lemon juice, preferably fresh
•	zest of 1 lemon, optional
¼ tsp	ground ginger
¼ tsp	sea salt
¼ tsp	coarsely ground black pepper
¼ cup	coarse ground mustard
¼ cup	dark brown sugar, packed

1. **Prepare the corned beef:** To a large pot over medium-low heat, add corned beef with water to cover. Add vinegar and pickling spice. Bring to a boil; cook for 1½ hours. Alternatively, place meat into a baking pan with 1-inch boiling water. Add vinegar and pickling spice. Seal tightly with foil. Bake at 350°F for 1½ hours.

2. Remove meat from water or baking pan. Allow to cool slightly. Slice across the grain.

3. Preheat oven to 350°F. Set out a 9x13-inch baking pan or oven-to-table cookware.

4. **Prepare the glaze:** In a small bowl, whisk together glaze ingredients until well combined.

5. Place sliced corned beef into prepared pan. Pour apple juice around the meat. Pour glaze over meat. Cover pan with foil. Bake 45 minutes.

—Note

Red currant jam can be substituted with raspberry or blackberry jam.

LOW AND SLOW FLANKEN ROAST

Meat   **YIELDS** *6-10 servings*

This maple BBQ roast is one of my family's favorites and is a no-brainer. I know when I serve this it's going to be a sure-fire hit.

1 (3-5-lb) flanken roast

• olive oil, to coat

Maple BBQ Sauce

1 Tbsp canola oil

2 Tbsp minced onion *or* ¼ **small** onion, diced

4 cloves garlic, crushed

1 cup ketchup

½ cup pure maple syrup

3 Tbsp apple cider vinegar

2 Tbsp dark brown sugar

2 tsp ground mustard

• black pepper, to taste

• sea salt, to taste

Dry Rub

2 Tbsp dark brown sugar

1 Tbsp kosher salt

1 Tbsp garlic powder

1 Tbsp chili powder

1 tsp ground mustard

1 tsp smoked paprika

¼ tsp cayenne pepper

¼ tsp coarsely ground black pepper

1. **Prepare the maple BBQ sauce:** In a skillet, over medium heat, heat oil. Add onion and garlic. Brown until fragrant.

2. Add remaining sauce ingredients. Bring to a boil. Reduce heat; simmer for 15 minutes. Refrigerate sauce to cool.

3. **Prepare the dry rub:** In small bowl, combine rub ingredients.

4. Preheat oven to 450°F. Set out a 9x13-inch baking pan. Set out 2 sheets of foil, each large enough to line the pan and come together at the top. Place one over the other, to form a plus sign. Place foil into baking pan.

5. Coat flanken roast with olive oil. Coat entire roast with dry rub. Place roast on sheets of foil.

6. Bake, uncovered, for 20-30 minutes. Remove from oven. Lower oven temperature to 325°F.

7. Spread maple BBQ sauce over roast. Seal foil into a tent, in all 4 directions, left to right, right to left, top to bottom, and bottom to top, without touching the meat. Bake for 3½-4 hours. Alternatively, bake the roast at 225°F overnight for 10-12 hours.

BRAISED BOURBON RIBS

Meat   **YIELDS** *5-6 servings*

No need to worry; although there is actual bourbon in the recipe, the alcohol has plenty of time to burn off during the slow cooking process. What's left is a slightly smoky flavor that pairs perfectly with all the other ingredients. Get ready to use your hands when you dig into these soft, succulent ribs.

10	spare ribs

Spice Rub

3 Tbsp	dark brown sugar
1 Tbsp	garlic powder
1 Tbsp	chili powder
1 tsp	ground mustard
1 tsp	smoked paprika
½ Tbsp	kosher salt
¼ tsp	coarsely ground black pepper
¼ tsp	cayenne pepper

Bourbon Glaze

½ cup	bourbon
½ cup	dark brown sugar
¼ cup	pure maple syrup
¼ cup	prepared white horseradish
¼ cup	apple cider vinegar
2 Tbsp	Dijon mustard
2 Tbsp	fish-free Worcestershire sauce

1. **Prepare the spice rub:** In a small bowl. combine spice rub ingredients.

2. Place ribs into a 9x13-inch pan. Season with spice rub.

3. **Prepare the bourbon glaze:** In a small bowl, whisk together glaze ingredients.

4. Pour glaze over the ribs. Cover pan tightly with foil; marinate overnight in the fridge. (If pressed for time, marinate for at least 30 minutes on the counter.)

5. Preheat oven to 325°F.

6. Bake, covered, for 2½-3 hours.

TEXAS BBQ BRISKET

Meat   *YIELDS 6-8 servings*

A common question I receive is how to properly cook a brisket that isn't dry. The key is in the liquid and in proper timing. This Texas BBQ sauce yields a brisket that is smoky, tender, and juicy. Any leftovers (unlikely) can be used in sandwiches or tacos, too.

1 (3-4-lb)	brisket
1 Tbsp	olive oil
4 cloves	garlic, crushed

Rub

2 Tbsp	dark brown sugar
2 tsp	smoked paprika
1 tsp	onion powder
1 tsp	kosher salt
¾ tsp	ground mustard
½ tsp	coarsely ground black pepper

Texas BBQ Sauce

1 (12-oz) jar	chili sauce
½ cup	ketchup
½ cup	vinegar
½ cup	dark brown sugar
2 cloves	garlic, crushed
2 Tbsp	fish-free Worcestershire sauce
2 tsp	onion powder
2 tsp	ground mustard
1 tsp	coarsely ground black pepper

1. Preheat oven to 325°F.

2. Pat roast dry with paper towels. Coat with olive oil. Spread garlic over roast.

3. **Prepare the rub:** Combine all rub ingredients in a small cup. Rub over entire roast. If time allows, allow roast to rest for 30 minutes.

4. **Prepare the Texas BBQ sauce:** In a medium bowl, combine all BBQ sauce ingredients.

5. Pour sauce over roast. Cover pan tightly with foil. Bake for 2½ hours. (See Tip.)

Tip

Caterer's secret: To reheat, place cold sliced meat into a pan. In a saucepan, bring pan juices to a boil; pour over meat. The meat will be ready to serve and won't fall apart.

Sides

SPINACH MUSHROOM RICE

Pareve YIELDS *6 servings*

2 cups	water + **2 tsp** pareve beef broth powder
1 cup	basmati rice
2 Tbsp	olive oil
1 large	onion, diced
6 cloves	garlic, crushed
8 oz	shiitake mushrooms *or* mushrooms of choice, sliced
2 handfuls	fresh baby spinach leaves
1 tsp	kosher salt
¼ tsp	coarsely ground black pepper
½ tsp	dried thyme
½ tsp	garlic powder
½ tsp	umami powder, optional but recommended

My sister-in-law Esther Leah called me all excited that Erev Shabbos had come and she realized she hadn't made a side dish. With no time to shop, she literally used whatever she had on hand and hoped for the best. Well, the results were so spectacular she had to share. Tried it, loved it, and had to pass it on to you!

1. In a 2-quart saucepan, over medium-high heat, bring water and broth powder to a boil. Add rice. Lower the heat, cover the saucepan, and simmer rice for 20 minutes. Remove from heat.

2. While the rice is cooking, heat olive oil in a large skillet over medium-high heat. Add onion and garlic; sauté for 5-7 minutes, until slightly golden. Add mushrooms; cook until softened and all liquid is absorbed, about 5 minutes. Add spinach leaves and spices. Cook, stirring, until spinach is just wilted.

3. Combine prepared rice with vegetables. Serve warm.

— Note —

Umami powder, made from mushrooms, is available in many supermarkets.

OVEN-BAKED SPANISH ORZO

Pareve **YIELDS** *4-6 servings*

2 Tbsp	olive oil
½ large	onion, diced, *or* **2 cubes** frozen caramelized onions
1	red pepper, diced
1	yellow pepper, diced
1	orange pepper, diced
2 cloves	garlic, crushed, *or* **2 cubes** frozen garlic
2 tsp	dried oregano
1 tsp	kosher salt
pinch	cayenne pepper, or more to taste
3 Tbsp	tomato paste
1½ cups	uncooked orzo
1 (14-oz) can	diced fire-roasted tomatoes
2 cups	vegetable broth *or* **2 cups** water + **2 tsp** pareve consommé powder

Orzo and sautéed vegetables that skip the stovetop? Yup! Instead, you'll combine all the ingredients in a baking dish and toss in the oven for 25 minutes. Yes, that's really it. It's so simple, you'll surely make it again and again.

1. Preheat oven to high broil.

2. Place oil, onions, and peppers into a 9x13-inch baking pan. Broil for 10 minutes, uncovered, stirring after 5 minutes.

3. Set oven temperature to 400°F.

4. Add remaining ingredients to the pan. Bake, covered, for 15-20 minutes, until orzo is soft and liquid is mostly absorbed. Remove from oven. As orzo cools, remaining liquid will be absorbed. Serve warm.

GNOCCHI AND PASTRAMI

Meat **YIELDS** *6 servings*

With the addition of sauteed onions and pastrami, this is a novel twist on traditional shlishkes.

2 Tbsp	canola oil
1 large	onion, diced
1 (6-oz) package	sliced pastrami, diced
4 cloves	garlic, crushed
⅓ cup	seasoned panko crumbs
1 (16-oz) package	mini gnocchi
¼ tsp	sea salt
⅛ tsp	coarsely ground black pepper
¼ tsp	onion powder

1. In a large skillet, over medium heat, heat oil. Add onion; sauté until golden, stirring occasionally, about 15 minutes. Raise heat to high; add pastrami. Continue sautéing, stirring occasionally, for an additional 5 minutes. Add crushed garlic and panko crumbs; heat until garlic becomes fragrant, about 1 minute, stirring well to combine. Remove from heat; set aside.

2. Fill a 3-quart pot three-quarters-full with water. Bring to a rolling boil over high heat. Add mini gnocchi; boil for 3 minutes. Drain in a colander; run under cold water, shaking the gnocchi in the colander so they don't stick to one another.

3. Add gnocchi to the onion-pastrami mixture. Stir well to combine. Serve warm.

SMOKY CAULIFLOWER BITES

Pareve   YIELDS *8 servings*

5 Tbsp	olive oil
1 tsp	smoked paprika
½ tsp	sea salt
¼ tsp	crushed red pepper flakes
pinch	black pepper
2 lb	fresh or frozen cauliflower florets (see Note)
2 Tbsp	honey
1½ tsp	lemon juice

Smoked paprika and crushed red pepper flakes give extra depth to a simple side of roasted cauliflower. Drizzling the honey and lemon during the final roast takes it over the top. This will definitely become your new favorite.

1. Preheat oven to 450°F. Line a baking sheet with parchment paper.

2. In a large resealable bag, combine olive oil, paprika, salt, red pepper flakes, and pepper. Add cauliflower florets, seal bag, and shake until all pieces are well coated.

3. Transfer cauliflower to prepared baking sheet. Bake for 20 minutes.

4. Combine honey and lemon juice. Drizzle over cauliflower; toss to coat. Return to oven; bake an additional 15 minutes.

Note

If using frozen cauliflower, run under hot water until fully defrosted, drain well, and place on paper towels to dry.

Tip

Steps 1-2 can be done the night before and then cauliflower can be refrigerated in the resealable bag until ready to bake.

GLAZED ZUCCHINI SPEARS

Pareve   **YIELDS** *6-8 servings*

As I was looking through my archives, I came across my dog-eared recipe card for ratatouille. Remembering how popular it was in my home, I decided to make an updated version. After some trial and error, a new star was born.

4-5 medium   zucchini, not peeled

2 Tbsp   olive oil, divided

•   kosher salt, to taste

•   coarsely ground black pepper, to taste

Sweet and Sour Sauce

¼ cup   honey

2 Tbsp   low sodium soy sauce

2 Tbsp   duck sauce

2 Tbsp   ketchup

1 Tbsp   olive oil

1 Tbsp   vinegar

3 cloves   garlic, crushed

1. Wash zucchini; pat dry. Slice each zucchini in half lengthwise and then widthwise, then slice each quarter into thirds lengthwise, yielding 12 spears per zucchini.

2. Preheat a large frying pan over medium heat with 1 tablespoon olive oil. Place zucchini spears in a single layer over the entire bottom of the pan. (You will have to do this in batches.) Sprinkle with salt and pepper. Cook for 3 minutes, until golden. Turn each spear; cook an additional 2 minutes. Transfer to a serving dish. Repeat, adding the second tablespoon olive oil to the pan as necessary, until all zucchini spears are browned.

3. **Prepare the sweet and sour sauce:** In a small bowl, combine all sweet and sour sauce ingredients.

4. Pour sauce into the same frying pan; bring to a boil. Turn off heat. Pour sauce over prepared zucchini. Serve warm or at room temperature.

— Note —

These spears taste fabulous freshly made. If there are any leftovers, they'll remain fresh beautifully in the refrigerator for 3 days.

HERBED CAULIFLOWER RICE

Pareve   YIELDS *6-8 servings*

This herbed cauliflower rice is not only healthy and low-carb, it is also quick, easy to put together, and packed full of flavor.

½ cup	slivered almonds
2 Tbsp	extra light olive oil
3 cloves	garlic, crushed
16 oz	riced cauliflower, fresh or frozen (see Note)
¼ tsp	kosher salt
¼ tsp	onion powder
⅛ tsp	coarsely ground black pepper
¼ cup	fresh parsley leaves, chopped
¼ cup	fresh dill leaves, chopped
1 Tbsp	lemon juice

1. Prepare a piece of foil.

2. Place almonds into a large skillet over medium heat. Stir almonds until fragrant and lightly toasted, 3-5 minutes. Using a slotted spoon, transfer nuts to prepared foil to cool.

3. Return skillet to heat. Add olive oil and garlic. Cook, stirring, until fragrant, about 30 seconds. Add riced cauliflower, salt, onion powder, and pepper. Cook 7-10 minutes, stirring occasionally.

4. Remove skillet from heat. Stir in chopped herbs, lemon juice, and toasted almonds. Serve warm.

Note
If using frozen riced cauliflower: place in a colander and run under warm water. Drain well. You may need additional cooking time to ensure all liquid is absorbed.

Tip
Rice will stay fresh in the refrigerator in an airtight container for 3 days.

STICKY GREEN BEANS

Pareve   YIELDS *6-8 servings*

Glazed, sweet, tangy, and topped with crispy shallots, these are oh-so-addictive and make for the ultimate side dish.

1½-2 lb	green beans, trimmed
⅓ cup	silan
3 Tbsp	red wine vinegar
3 Tbsp	olive oil
1¼ tsp	kosher salt
¾ tsp	coarsely ground black pepper
•	canola oil, for frying
¼ cup	sliced shallots

1. Bring a 6-quart pot of water to a rolling boil over high heat. Add green beans to boiling water; blanch for 3 minutes. To help beans retain their bright green color, plunge them into ice water to stop the cooking process. Drain green beans; set aside to cool slightly.

2. In a small saucepan, combine silan and red wine vinegar. Bring to a boil; reduce heat and simmer, without stirring, for 4 minutes. Remove from heat; cool for 5 minutes.

3. Toss green beans with olive oil, salt, and pepper.

4. In a 1-quart saucepan over medium-high heat, heat ½-inch canola oil. Place shallots into heated oil; fry until golden. Use a slotted spoon to transfer shallots to a paper towel to drain.

5. Toss green beans with silan mixture and fried shallots.

— Note —

Green beans can be blanched one day in advance; refrigerate once cool.

CARAMELIZED MUSHROOMS

Pareve   YIELDS *6 servings*

3 Tbsp	olive oil
4 cloves	garlic, crushed
24 oz	baby bella or white mushrooms, quartered
¼ cup	red wine vinegar
2 Tbsp	fish-free Worcestershire sauce
3 Tbsp	ketchup
pinch	kosher salt
pinch	black pepper

While hesitant to make another mushroom dish, I decided I just couldn't leave these out. Tender and delicious, these mushrooms are cooked until sticky and golden brown. With their delectable earthy flavor, these go with pretty much everything.

1. In a skillet, over medium-low heat, heat olive oil. Add garlic; stir for 30 seconds, until fragrant. Raise heat to medium. Add mushrooms; cook until they begin to release liquid.

2. Stir in red wine vinegar. Raise heat to medium-high. Add Worcestershire sauce, ketchup, salt, and pepper. Stir occasionally until liquid has completely evaporated and the mushrooms are glazed, about 15 minutes. Remove from heat.

---Tip---

This recipe can be easily halved or doubled.

SUGAR SNAP PEA STIR FRY

Pareve   **YIELDS** *6-8 servings*

Say hello to this super easy sugar snap pea with portobello dish. This is my go-to healthy vegetable side when I don't have a lot of time for preparing.

4 Tbsp	canola oil, divided
6 oz	sliced portobello mushrooms
1	red onion, sliced
3 cloves	garlic, crushed
10 oz	sugar snap peas, trimmed
1 tsp	ground ginger
•	kosher salt, to taste
•	black pepper, to taste
2 Tbsp	honey
2 tsp	low sodium soy sauce
1 tsp	sesame oil
1 cup	cashews, whole, optional

1. Heat a large skillet over medium-high heat for about 30 seconds. Add 3 tablespoon canola oil, swirl it around the pan. Add mushrooms, stir to coat, and allow to begin to brown, about 1 minute. Add onion and garlic; stir fry for 3-4 minutes.

2. Add remaining tablespoon oil. Add sugar snap peas, ginger, salt, and pepper. Stir for 1 minute. Add honey, soy sauce, and sesame oil. Toss for 1-2 minutes until sugar snap peas are crisp-tender and liquid is reduced to a glaze. Add additional salt and pepper to taste. Sprinkle with cashews, if using.

BLACKENED BROCCOLI

Pareve   YIELDS *4 servings*

Crispy, blackened, and extra delicious, this oven roasting showcases broccoli at its best. For an extra garlic kick, add minced garlic to the spice mix, as pictured.

24 oz	fresh or frozen broccoli florets *or* baby broccoli (broccolini)
¼ cup	olive oil
1 tsp	garlic powder
½ tsp	onion powder
½ tsp	kosher salt
¼ tsp	ground mustard
¼ tsp	chili powder
⅛ tsp	cayenne pepper
½ tsp	garlic salt, optional
•	minced garlic, optional

1. Preheat oven to 450°F. Line a baking sheet with parchment paper.

2. In a large bowl, combine oil and spices. Add broccoli; toss until evenly coated.

3. Transfer broccoli to prepared baking sheet in a single layer.

4. Bake 15-20 minutes. Adjust seasoning if necessary. Serve immediately.

─ Note ─

If using frozen broccoli, either thaw completely or run under water and drain well.

SOY-GLAZED EDAMAME

Pareve   YIELDS *4-6 servings*

I made these sweet and spicy soy glazed edamame for a tasty snack. My family stood around the kitchen counter and devoured the entire bowl in a matter of minutes.

1 (1-lb) bag frozen edamame in pods

2 Tbsp olive oil *or* **1 Tbsp** olive oil and **1 Tbsp** sesame oil

1 tsp low sodium soy sauce

1 tsp kosher salt

¼ tsp garlic powder

⅛ tsp coarsely ground black pepper

1 Tbsp sweet chili sauce

dash hot sauce, optional

1. Prepare edamame according to package directions. Drain well; set aside.

2. In a skillet over high heat, heat oil. When oil is hot, add edamame; stir fry for 3 minutes. Add soy sauce, salt, garlic powder, and pepper. Remove from heat. Stir in sweet chili and hot sauces.

3. Serve immediately or refrigerate. Enjoy hot or cold!

JAPANESE YAM SPEARS

Pareve   YIELDS *24 wedges*

Crispy outside, creamy inside, and lightly spiced, oh-so-nice, these are the absolute best yam spears out there.

3 medium	Japanese yams, peeled (see Note)
3 Tbsp	olive oil
¼ cup	dark brown sugar
1 Tbsp	lemon juice
1 tsp	cinnamon
½ tsp	chili powder
pinch	cayenne pepper

1. Preheat oven to 400°F. Line a baking sheet with parchment paper.

2. Cut potatoes in half lengthwise. Slice each half into 4 spears.

3. In a large bowl, combine olive oil, brown sugar, lemon juice, cinnamon, chili powder, and cayenne pepper. Add yam wedges to bowl; toss to coat.

4. Place wedges in a single layer on prepared baking sheet. Bake for 20 minutes.

5. Remove from oven. Turn wedges over. Return to oven; bake an additional 10-15 minutes. Serve warm or at room temperature.

—Note—

Japanese yams are also known as Korean yams or Oriental yams. Sweet potatoes can be used if Japanese yams are not available.

SALT-BAKED
GARLIC ROASTED POTATOES

Pareve YIELDS *8 servings*

Here is the secret to the best baked potatoes that yields the fluffiest, buttery soft, most delicious potatoes that will leave everyone asking for more.

2¼ cups	kosher salt
1½-2 lb	baby or fingerling potatoes
¼ cup	olive oil
6 cloves	garlic, crushed
2 Tbsp	fresh parsley, chopped, *or* **2 tsp** dried parsley flakes
1 Tbsp	dried minced onion
1 tsp	kosher salt
¾ tsp	coarsely ground black pepper

1. Preheat oven to 350°F. Prepare a 9x13-inch baking pan.

2. Pour salt into prepared pan. Rinse and dry potatoes; press them into salt. Cover with foil. Bake for 1 hour.

3. Meanwhile, in a small bowl, combine olive oil, garlic, parsley, onion, salt, and pepper. Set aside.

4. Remove pan from oven. Lift potatoes from salt; brush off any excess salt. Discard salt; rinse pan. Return potatoes to pan.

5. Brush potatoes with garlic-herb mixture. Return to oven, uncovered; bake an additional 15-20 minutes.

— Note

This is a totally new potato experience. During the baking process, moisture escapes from the potato and is absorbed by the salt. The potato then reabsorbs that moisture from the salt, helping to achieve the perfect baked potato.

BRITTLE-TOPPED SWEET POTATO PIE

Pareve   YIELDS *8-10 servings*

This is a traditional sweet potato pie topped with a brittle-like layer. Familiar, yet somehow much better.

3 medium	sweet potatoes, peeled and cubed
½ cup	nondairy milk
¼ cup	canola oil
¼ cup	sugar
¼ cup	pure maple syrup
2	eggs
1 tsp	pure vanilla extract
½ tsp	cinnamon

Brittle Topping

½ cup	sugar
⅓ cup	flour
3 Tbsp	canola oil
1½ tsp	cinnamon

1. Preheat oven to 350°F. Prepare a 9-inch oven-to-table baking dish.

2. **Prepare the brittle topping:** Combine topping ingredients in a small bowl by hand or with a fork until fine crumbs form. Set aside.

3. Add sweet potatoes to a medium saucepan; add water to cover. Over high heat, bring sweet potatoes to a boil. Boil for 20 minutes, until soft. Drain; mash thoroughly.

4. Add remaining ingredients to mashed sweet potatoes. Mix until well combined.

5. Pour mixture into prepared baking dish. Sprinkle with brittle topping.

6. Bake 50 minutes.

— Note —

This recipe is freezer friendly!

— Variation —

Alternatively, you can prepare this recipe as mini pies. Divide mixture between 9 ramekins. Divide topping between the ramekins. Bake for 30 minutes.

STICKY SMASHED POTATOES

Meat or Pareve

YIELDS *4-6 servings*

1½-2 lb	baby potatoes
2 Tbsp	olive oil
2 cups	chicken broth *or* **2 cups** water + **2 tsp** consommé powder
•	chopped chives, for garnish, optional

Honey-Balsamic Glaze

6 Tbsp	balsamic vinegar
6 Tbsp	honey
6 Tbsp	low sodium soy sauce
1 Tbsp	spicy brown mustard
2 cloves	garlic, crushed

There's a serious chance that only half of these will make it to the dinner table.

1. Rinse potatoes; pat dry. Place into a large skillet. Add olive oil; place pan over medium-high heat. Allow potatoes to pan-fry, turning them occasionally, 5-7 minutes, until lightly browned on all sides. Add broth. Cover lightly; cook for 10-20 minutes. Fork test for tenderness. (Larger potatoes will take longer to cook through.) Once tender, turn off heat. Drain off any remaining liquid.

2. Use the back of a large spoon to smash each potato in the pan.

3. **Prepare the honey-balsamic glaze:** In a small bowl, combine glaze ingredients.

4. Brush glaze over potatoes. Pour remaining glaze into pan. Over medium-low heat, simmer potatoes in the glaze. This will intensify the flavor and allow the glaze to become thick and sticky.

5. Baste with glaze before serving. Garnish with chopped chives, if desired.

HONEY APPLE MUFFINS

Pareve   YIELDS *16 muffins*

½ cup	oil
⅓ cup	light brown sugar
1 Tbsp	vanilla sugar
2	eggs
⅓ cup	honey
2 cups	flour
2 tsp	baking powder
1 tsp	baking soda
½ tsp	cinnamon
½ tsp	sea salt
½ cup	apple juice
2	firm apples (Pink Lady, Gala, or Granny Smith), peeled and finely diced

After much trial and error, I'm happy to share these honey apple muffins: super easy to make, perfect for Rosh Hashanah and all year round, absolutely irresistible, and a great way to use those extra apples you have around.

1. Preheat oven to 375°F. Coat 16 muffin cups with baking spray or line with muffin liners.

2. In a bowl of an electric mixer, on medium speed, beat oil and sugars until combined. Add eggs; beat until batter becomes light and fluffy. Add honey and beat until combined.

3. Add remaining ingredients except apples. Beat until just incorporated. Fold in diced apples.

4. Divide evenly between prepared muffin cups. Bake for 18-20 minutes. Cool in muffin cups for 5 minutes. Remove from muffin cups; cool completely.

BLUEBERRY PLUM COBBLER

Pareve YIELDS *8 servings*

A sweet and tart mixture of fresh blueberries and plums, under a crisp, never-fail cobbler topping.

Crumble

½ cup	old-fashioned oats
½ cup	flour
½ cup	tea biscuit crumbs (about 11 tea biscuits, crushed)
½ cup	light brown sugar
4 Tbsp	canola oil

Filling

6	plums, sliced ¼-inch-thick
1½ cups	blueberries
3 Tbsp	sugar
1 Tbsp	vanilla sugar
1 Tbsp	cornstarch
1 Tbsp	lemon juice

1. Preheat oven to 350°F. Coat a 10-inch oven-to-table baking dish with cooking spray.

2. **Prepare the crumble:** In a medium bowl, combine crumble ingredients. Set aside.

3. In a large bowl, combine filling ingredients.

4. Transfer filling into prepared baking dish. Top with crumble mixture.

5. Bake for 40-45 minutes on center rack.

Tip

To avoid a mess in the oven, place the baking dish onto a baking sheet before placing it in the oven; this will catch any overflow of fruit juices.

Variation

Alternatively, divide crumble and filling between ramekins (as pictured). Reduce baking time to 30-35 minutes.

Desserts

CHOCOLATE MOUSSE CREAM PUFF RING

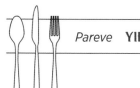

Pareve **YIELDS** *8 servings*

Light and delicious, this mousse is divine and my go-to chocolate mousse recipe. Combined with the airy cream puff it becomes truly outstanding.

Cream Puffs

½ cup	margarine (1 stick)
1 cup	water
½ tsp	sea salt
1 cup	flour
4	eggs

3-Ingredient Chocolate Mousse

8 oz	quality baking chocolate, chopped
⅔ cup	light corn syrup
2 cups	nondairy whipping cream, divided

Chocolate Ganache

3½ oz	quality chocolate, chopped
2 Tbsp	light corn syrup
⅓ cup	nondairy whipping cream

1. Set out a baking sheet. Using a 7-inch plate as a guide, use a marker to trace a circle onto a piece of parchment paper. Turn the paper over, place onto baking sheet, lightly grease, and dust with flour.

2. **Prepare the cream puffs:** In a 2-quart sauce pan, over medium heat, heat margarine, water, and salt until mixture comes to a boil. Remove from heat.

3. Add flour; vigorously mix with a wooden spoon until mixture forms a ball and leaves the side of the pan.

4. Preheat oven to 400°F.

5. Add eggs to the flour mixture, one at a time, whisking well after each addition, until smooth and shiny. Cool mixture slightly.

6. Using a large spoon and spatula, drop batter in mounds onto prepared baking sheet, just inside the marked circle, touching slightly, to form a ring. Bake 40 minutes, until golden and firm. Remove from oven; allow to cool.

7. **Prepare the 3-ingredient chocolate mousse:** Place chopped chocolate into a 3-quart saucepan. Add corn syrup; place over low heat. Stir until mixture melts and is smooth. Remove from heat. Stir in ½ cup nondairy whipping cream. Refrigerate 15 minutes.

8. In the bowl of an electric mixer, beat remaining 1½ cups whipping cream until stiff peaks form. Fold in chocolate mixture until completely combined.

9. With a sharp knife, slice cream puff ring in half horizontally, as if slicing a bagel. Spread mousse over the bottom half of the ring. Replace top; refrigerate.

10. **Prepare the chocolate ganache:** In a small saucepan over low heat, heat chocolate and corn syrup until melted and smooth. Remove from heat. Stir in whipping cream.

11. Spread ganache over cream puff ring. Refrigerate or freeze until ready to serve.

STRAWBERRY SHORTCAKE

Pareve **YIELDS** *8 servings*

This light as a feather strawberry shortcake is simplified without compromising on quality or flavor, for the ultimate shortcake experience. I chose to use a genoise as the cake base, as it achieves the fluffiness of a classic sponge cake without having to separate eggs.

Genoise

6	eggs, room temperature
1 cup	sugar
1 cup	flour
¼ cup	canola oil
1 tsp	pure vanilla extract
½ tsp	lemon zest, optional
½ tsp	sea salt

Strawberry Sauce

2 lb	frozen strawberries, defrosted in a colander set over a bowl
1 cup	strawberry liquid (see Note)
¼ cup	sugar
1 Tbsp	lemon juice
1 tsp	cornstarch

Whipping Cream

16 oz	nondairy whipping cream, chilled
¼ cup	powdered sugar
1 tsp	pure vanilla extract
•	fresh strawberries, optional, for garnish

Note

For strawberry liquid, place frozen strawberries into a colander set over a bowl; allow to thaw until fully defrosted. As strawberries thaw, they will release liquid. Measure the liquid; add water to reach 1 cup.

1. **Prepare the genoise:** Preheat oven to 350°F. Generously spray 2 (9-inch) round pans with baking spray with flour. Cut 2 pieces of parchment paper into 9-inch circles and line the bottom of the pans. Coat parchment paper with baking spray with flour. This will help release the cake after baking.

2. Warm eggs by placing them into a bowl and covering them with hot water for 1 minute, no longer. If using a metal mixing bowl, run the bowl under hot water and dry well. This is a very important step that will help achieve volume when beating the eggs.

3. Remove eggs from water, dry, and add eggs to the bowl of an electric mixer fitted with the whisk attachment. Beat on low speed to combine eggs; increase to high speed. Slowly add sugar; continue to beat for a total of 8 minutes until thick and high in volume.

4. Sift flour into egg mixture, one-third at a time. Fold with a spatula after each addition until incorporated, taking care not to over-mix. Be sure to scrape spatula from the bottom to ensure that no flour pockets remain.

5. In a small bowl combine oil, vanilla, zest (if using), and salt; add to batter. Fold in until well combined.

6. Divide batter evenly between prepared pans. Place both pans on one oven rack; bake for 15 minutes. Rotate pans on the rack; bake for an additional 5-10 minutes, until top is golden. Release and transfer cakes to cooling rack by inverting pans; remove parchment paper. (Run a knife around the edges if necessary.) Turn right-side-up to cool. Allow cakes to cool. Cakes may be frozen at this point; defrost before assembling.

7. **Prepare the strawberry sauce:** In a 3-quart saucepan, over medium heat, combine sauce ingredients; bring to a boil. (Strawberries can be pureed before making the strawberry sauce if a smooth consistency is preferred.) Stir until boiling and thickened. Remove from heat. Allow to cool. Sauce may be made up to 2 days in advance.

8. **Prepare the whipping cream:** In a large bowl, beat whipping cream until stiff peaks form. Add powdered sugar and vanilla. Beat until combined.

9. **To assemble:** Spread half the strawberry sauce over 1 cake layer. Top with half the whipped cream. Place second cake on top. Pipe whipped cream onto cake. Fill with remaining strawberry sauce. Refrigerate for 1 hour before serving to set. Garnish with fresh strawberries, as pictured, if desired.

—Tip—————————————————————
Sifting the flour is very important for this recipe, as it will ensure a light, fluffy cake.

—Note—————————————————————
This cake is freezer friendly. Allow to thaw completely before serving.

CINNABUN CHEESECAKE

Dairy **YIELDS** *10-12 servings*

This cheesecake is reminiscent of a delicious cinnamon bun paired with a thick and creamy cheesecake. With a ribbon of cinnamon running through it and topped off with the buttery cinnabun cookies, this is equally delectable as it is exquisite!

1 batch	Cinnabun Cookies (page 298), not baked

Cinnamon Filling

1 cup	light brown sugar, packed
6 Tbsp	flour
6 Tbsp	butter, melted
1 Tbsp	cinnamon

Cheesecake Filling

4 (8-oz) bars	cream cheese, at room temperature
1 cup	light brown sugar
1 Tbsp	pure vanilla extract
5	eggs, at room temperature
¾ cup	sour cream
⅓ cup	heavy cream

Cream Cheese Frosting

4 Tbsp	butter (½ stick), at room temperature
4 oz	cream cheese (½ bar)
½ tsp	pure vanilla extract
⅛ tsp	sea salt
2 cups	powdered sugar

1. **Prepare 1 batch cinnabun cookies.** Set aside half the unbaked cookies to use as the cheesecake crust. Bake remaining cookies as directed; reserve for garnish.

2. Preheat oven to 350°F.

3. **Prepare the cheesecake crust:** Grease sides and bottom of a 9-inch springform pan. Line the bottom with a circle of parchment paper. Place unbaked cinnabuns into the pan, covering most of the bottom. Bake for 12 minutes. Remove from oven; set aside to cool.

4. Lower oven temperature to 325°F.

5. **Prepare the cinnamon filling:** In a medium bowl, use a fork to thoroughly combine cinnamon filling ingredients. Set aside.

6. **Prepare the cheesecake filling:** Place cream cheese into the bowl of an electric mixer. Cream until completely smooth, scraping the bottom and sides of the bowl as needed. Add sugar; beat for 1 minute on low speed. Add vanilla. Add 1 egg at a time, allowing each egg to combine fully before adding the next (about 30 seconds each). Add sour cream and heavy cream. Beat until completely smooth.

7. Pour one-third of the cheesecake filling into cooled crust. Sprinkle with half the cinnamon filling. Add another third of the cheesecake filling, followed by remaining cinnamon filling. Top with remaining third of cheesecake filling. Wrap bottom and sides of springform pan with foil. Tap springform pan on the counter to release any air bubbles.

8. Fill a 9x13-inch baking pan with 2 inches water; place on the bottom rack of oven. Place springform pan on the center rack. Bake for 45 minutes.

9. Turn off oven, open oven door, and allow cheesecake to cool in the oven for 1 hour. Remove cake from oven; chill overnight in the fridge.

10. **Once the cheesecake has set, prepare the cream cheese frosting:** Add butter and cream cheese to the bowl of an electric mixer; beat until creamy and lump-free. Add vanilla and salt, beating until combined. Add powdered sugar, beating until combined. Spread over cake top with an offset spatula. Use reserved baked cinnabun cookies to garnish.

11. Optional: Sprinkle a very light coating of cinnamon over cheesecake.

FRESH FRUIT NACHOS

Pareve **YIELDS** *8-10 servings*

Everything about these layers of fresh fruit, cinnamon-sugar crisps, and sweet cream nachos is fabulous and they are a huge hit with everyone who tries them.

8 (6-inch)	flour tortillas
⅓ cup	oil
1 cup	sugar
2 tsp	vanilla sugar
2 tsp	cinnamon

Fruity Dipping Creams

24 oz	nondairy whipping cream
1 (7.5-oz) container	marshmallow creme
½ cup	blackberry pie filling or jam
½ cup	raspberry pie filling or jam
½ cup	lemon curd, lemon cream, or lemon pie filling

For serving

- fresh fruit of choice (blueberries, strawberries, kiwi, mango, etc.), cut into bite-size pieces

1. Preheat oven to 350°F. Line 3 baking sheets with parchment paper.

2. Place 3 tortillas on each baking sheet (the third sheet will have only 2). Brush each tortilla with oil.

3. In a small bowl, combine sugars and cinnamon. Sprinkle half the mixture generously over tortillas. Turn each tortilla over; brush second side with oil. Sprinkle with remaining sugar mixture.

4. With a sharp knife or pizza cutter, cut each tortilla into 8 wedges. Bake on center rack for 8-12 minutes or until lightly golden. Allow to cool. Store in an airtight container or resealable bag for up to 1 week.

5. **Prepare the fruity dipping creams:** In a large mixing bowl, beat whipping cream until stiff peaks form. Add marshmallow creme; beat until completely combined. Divide mixture evenly between 3 bowls. Add blackberry pie filling to one bowl, raspberry pie filling to the second, and lemon curd to the third. Stir until completely combined.

6. **To serve:** Spread nachos on a platter; arrange fresh fruit on platter, as pictured. Serve dipping creams in small bowls alongside or dolloped over the nachos. Alternatively, serve as individual portions.

RASPBERRY LIME CHEESECAKE PIE

This creamy dessert perfectly balances tart lime with sweet cheesecake. A one-of-a-kind show-stopping dessert that will have everyone requesting doubles.

Pareve

YIELDS *6-8 servings per pie*

3 (8-oz) tubs	nondairy cream cheese, room temperature
½ cup	nondairy sour cream
1½ cups	sugar
1 Tbsp	vanilla sugar
•	zest of 2 limes
4	eggs, at room temperature
⅓ cup	lime juice
½ cup	nondairy whipping cream
2 (6-oz)	prepared graham cracker crusts

Sour Cream Glaze

1½ cups	nondairy sour cream
2 Tbsp	sugar
1 Tbsp	lime juice
1 (1-1¼-oz) bag	freeze-dried raspberries, crushed, for garnish
•	lime wedges, for garnish, optional

1. Preheat oven to 325°F.

2. In the large bowl of an electric mixer, beat together cream cheese and sour cream until smooth. Scraping the sides to ensure a smooth batter, slowly add sugars and lime zest. Add 1 egg at a time, beating for 30 seconds between each addition. Beat in lime juice and whipping cream.

3. Divide batter between graham cracker crusts. Place pies on a baking sheet.

4. Place a 9x13-inch baking pan filled with 1-inch water on the lowest rack of oven. Place baking sheet with pies on the center rack. Bake 50-55 minutes, uncovered.

5. Turn off oven, open door, and leave pies in oven for 10 minutes. Remove pies from oven; cool in the refrigerator overnight.

6. **Prepare sour cream glaze:** Whisk glaze ingredients together until smooth and glossy. Divide between the 2 pies; spread evenly over the surface.

7. Garnish with crushed freeze-dried raspberries and lime wedges, if desired.

— Note —

This cheesecake pie is freezer friendly!

PLUM GALETTE

Pareve   **YIELDS** *8 servings*

1½ cups flour
3 Tbsp sugar
½ tsp sea salt
1 stick margarine, chilled, cut into ½-inch pieces
2 Tbsp ice water

Plum Filling

4 medium plums, halved, pitted and cut into ½-inch wedges
¼ cup sugar
2 Tbsp cornstarch
1 tsp lemon juice
• zest of 1 lemon
1 Tbsp vanilla sugar
½ cup seedless raspberry preserves, melted (see Note)
• water, for brushing
1-2 tsp turbinado sugar *or* white sugar, for sprinkling

With a flaky crust folded over juicy plums, this rustic plum galette makes a delightful dessert.

1. **Prepare the crust:** In a large bowl, combine flour, sugar, and salt. Add margarine; use your fingers to work it into the mixture until mixture resembles coarse crumbs. Sprinkle water over mixture, working it in, until dough has formed. Shape dough into a ball, cover in plastic wrap, and refrigerate for 1 hour.

2. Preheat oven to 425°F.

3. **Prepare the plum filling:** In a medium bowl, combine plums, sugar, cornstarch, lemon juice, zest, and vanilla sugar; toss to combine. Set aside.

4. Remove dough from refrigerator. Prepare a baking sheet and 2 sheets of parchment paper. Lightly flour one sheet of parchment paper. Place disc of dough on paper. Place second sheet of parchment paper on dough. Roll dough into a 12-inch round. Transfer the rolled-out dough, with the parchment sheets, onto prepared baking sheet. Remove and discard top sheet of parchment paper.

5. Spread half the melted raspberry preserves onto the dough, leaving a 2-inch border all around. Working in from the outer edge of the circle, lay plum wedges on the preserves, slightly overlapping wedges. Work inward until all plums have been used. Place in freezer for 10 minutes to firm the dough.

6. Using the parchment paper as a guide, gently fold up the dough around the border, pleating approximately every 3 inches and pressing down lightly to secure, up and over the fruit.

7. Brush crust with water; sprinkle crust with turbinado sugar (which yields a fabulous crunch). Bake 35-40 minutes. Remove from oven. Brush remaining raspberry preserves over plums. Allow to cool before serving.

— Note —————————————————
To melt preserves, microwave for 10-15 seconds.

TIRIMASU TOWERS

Pareve **YIELDS** *10 servings*

1 (10-count) package	4x4-inch puff pastry squares
¼ cup	hot water
1 heaping tsp	coffee granules
2 Tbsp	amaretto
•	cocoa powder, for dusting

Tiramisu Custard

6	egg yolks
¾ cup	sugar
⅔ cup	nondairy milk
16 oz	nondairy cream cheese, at room temperature
3 Tbsp	amaretto

Whipped Topping

16 oz	nondairy whipping cream
¼ cup	powdered sugar

Creamy, rich, and bursting with bold coffee and amaretto flavors, tiramisu is one of my all-time favorite desserts. I really wanted to make a pareve version as luscious as dairy. The cream layers are so luxurious, the puff pastry so crispy, you will take pleasure in each and every bite.

1. Defrost puff pastry squares in the refrigerator until easy to handle.

2. Preheat oven to 375°F. Line 2 baking sheets with parchment paper; set out a third baking sheet without parchment paper.

3. Cut each square of puff pastry down the center. Place 10 halves on each prepared baking sheet. Using a fork, pierce the puff pastry halves on one lined baking sheets multiple times. Cover pierced pastry halves with a sheet of parchment paper. Top with unlined baking sheet. This will prevent pastry from puffing up, since they will serve as the base of the towers. Place baking sheet with the unpierced halves on the center rack of oven. Place covered baking sheet on the lower rack. Bake 15 minutes. Remove uncovered baking sheet; set aside to cool. Remove top baking sheet and parchment paper from pierced halves; bake for an additional 5 minutes or until golden. Remove from oven; set aside to cool.

4. **Prepare the tiramisu custard:** In a medium saucepan, whisk egg yolks and sugar until well blended. Whisk in nondairy milk (do not beat). Cook over medium heat, stirring occasionally, until mixture comes to a low boil. Boil gently for 1 minute. Remove from heat. Transfer to a bowl. Cover with a piece of plastic wrap directly on the custard. Refrigerate for 1 hour.

5. Place nondairy cream cheese into the bowl of an electric mixer fitted with the whisk attachment. Beat on low speed until smooth. Add custard; mix well. Add amaretto; mix until incorporated. Set aside or refrigerate.

6. **Prepare the whipped topping:** In a large bowl, beat whipping cream until stiff peaks form. Add powdered sugar and continue to beat until incorporated.

7. In a small bowl, combine hot water, coffee granules, and amaretto.

8. **To assemble:** Drizzle pierced puff pastry with 1 tablespoon coffee mixture. Top with custard; smooth into an even layer. Top with whipped cream; smooth into an even layer. Top with puffed pastry. Garnish with whipped cream. Dust with cocoa. Refrigerate to set.

SALTED CARAMEL PECAN PIE

Pareve **YIELDS** *6-8 servings*

Salted caramel and Viennese crunch add a deep, creamy caramel flavor that is a wonderful combination of sweet and salty and takes the classic pecan pie up a notch. Although it might sound intimidating, this is actually easy as pie and anyone can make it.

1 (9-inch) prepared graham cracker crust

8 Viennese crunch sticks, coarsely chopped

Salted Caramel Pecan Filling

1 cup sugar

⅓ cup light corn syrup

2½ Tbsp water

4 Tbsp margarine (½ stick), cubed and softened

½ tsp pure vanilla extract

½ cup nondairy whipping cream, at room temperature

½ tsp kosher salt

2 eggs

1 cup pecan halves

• Maldon salt flakes, for garnish

1. In a large skillet, over medium-high heat, cook sugar, corn syrup, and water without stirring, until honey colored (8-10 minutes). Remove from heat.

2. Add margarine, stirring until melted. Add vanilla. Gradually stir in nondairy whipping cream and salt. Pour mixture into a bowl; allow to cool for 30 minutes.

3. Preheat oven to 350°F.

4. Add eggs to cooled mixture, whisking until smooth. Stir in pecans.

5. Place chopped Viennese crunch into graham cracker crust. Pour pecan mixture over crunch.

6. Bake for 55 minutes. Cool for 1 hour. Garnish with Maldon salt flakes.

— Note —
This pairs well with vanilla ice cream.

— Variation —
You may substitute a frozen pie shell if you prefer a less sweet crust.

VANILLA RUM RAINBOW FRUIT SALAD

Dairy or Pareve

YIELDS *8-10 servings*

Fresh fruit tossed in a vanilla and rum laced light simple syrup.

6 cups assorted fresh fruit of choice, diced

Suggestions

- strawberries
- pineapple
- blueberries
- kiwi
- red grapes
- peaches
- plums
- pomegranate arils
- nectarines
- mangoes

Vanilla Rum Sauce

1½ cups sugar

¾ cup water

1 vanilla bean, split, *or* **1 tsp** pure vanilla extract

1 Tbsp rum, optional

- dairy or nondairy vanilla ice cream, for serving

1. **Prepare the vanilla rum sauce:** In a small pot, over medium heat, bring sugar, water, and vanilla bean to a low boil. (If using vanilla extract, add in Step 2 with the rum.) As soon as the liquid turns clear, remove pan from heat. Overcooking will cause the mixture to crystalize.

2. Allow mixture to cool. Add rum, if using.

3. **To assemble:** Fill a small bowl with diced fruit. Top with 1 tablespoon vanilla rum sauce. Serve with a scoop of vanilla ice cream.

BOSTON CREAM PIE CUPS

Pareve **YIELDS** *24 cups*

With its combination of sugar cookie base, creamy vanilla custard, and rich chocolate ganache, this is a decadent twist on an old favorite.

Sugar Cookie Cups

½ cup	margarine (1 stick), softened
1 cup	canola oil
1 cup	sugar
1 cup	powdered sugar
2	eggs, at room temperature
1 tsp	pure vanilla extract
4½ cups	flour
1 tsp	baking soda
1 tsp	cream of tartar

Custard Cream

1 cup	nondairy whipping cream
3	egg yolks
¼ cup	sugar
pinch	sea salt
2 Tbsp	flour
2 Tbsp	margarine
1 tsp	pure vanilla extract

Chocolate Ganache

3½ oz	good quality chocolate, finely chopped
2 Tbsp	light corn syrup
⅓ cup	nondairy whipping cream
•	Maldon sea salt flakes, for sprinkling

Note

This recipe is freezer friendly.

---

1. **Prepare the sugar cookie cups:** Preheat oven to 375°F. Prepare 2 (12-cup) muffin pans.

2. In the large bowl of an electric mixer fitted with the cookie paddle(s), beat together margarine, oil, and sugars until combined. Beat in eggs, 1 at a time, until they are completely combined and batter is slightly fluffy. Beat in vanilla. Gradually add flour, baking soda, and cream of tartar.

3. Fill each muffin cup with ¼ cup batter (I used a medium cookie scoop to measure); pat each scoop flat in the cup.

4. Bake for 13 minutes, until lightly golden. Remove from oven; press the center of each tart with a shot glass, creating a deep indentation. Allow to cool completely. Slide a knife around the edges of each tart to loosen; remove to a cooling rack. Cookie cups may be frozen at this point if made in advance.

5. **Prepare the custard cream:** In a medium saucepan over medium heat, heat whipping cream until it begins to simmer (bubbles will begin to form at the edges).

6. Meanwhile, in a medium bowl, whisk together egg yolks, sugar, and salt until combined. Add flour, whisking to combine. Remove whipping cream from heat. Slowly whisk ½ cup whipping cream into the egg yolk mixture to temper (and avoid curdling the eggs).

7. Pour tempered yolk mixture into the saucepan with remaining whipping cream. Return saucepan to the stove over medium heat. Cook, stirring constantly, for 1 minute as the mixture thickens.

8. Lower heat to medium-low; simmer, whisking constantly, until bubbles burst to the surface (2-3 minutes). Add margarine and vanilla. Stir until melted and combined. Transfer custard to a bowl.

9. Lightly spray a piece of plastic wrap with cooking spray; press gently directly onto the custard surface. Refrigerate for at least 2 hours or up to 24 hours.

10. **Prepare the chocolate ganache:** In a small saucepan, over low heat, melt together chocolate and corn syrup, stirring until smooth. Remove from heat; stir in whipping cream. Allow mixture to sit for 1 minute. Whisk until combined and smooth, for about 30 seconds. Allow mixture to sit, whisking every minute until it thickens slightly (about 5 minutes total).

11. **To assemble:** Fill each cup with custard cream. Using an offset spatula or the back of a spoon, smooth 1 teaspoon chocolate ganache over custard.

12. Chill before serving.

VANILLA FUDGE
ICE CREAM PIE

Pareve   **YIELDS** *8 servings*

What's black and white and gone in a minute? Definitely this vanilla fudge ice cream cake!

Crust

⅓ cup	margarine, melted
½ cup	dark brown sugar, packed
½ cup	ground almonds *or* filberts
2 Tbsp	cocoa
1 Tbsp	pure vanilla extract
1¼ cups	old-fashioned oats

Vanilla Ice Cream

8 oz	nondairy whipping cream
2	eggs
½ cup	light corn syrup
2 tsp	pure vanilla extract

Chocolate Fudge

1 (3.7-oz) packet	chocolate pudding (not instant)
¾ cup	water
¼ cup	oil
¾ cup	light corn syrup

1. Preheat oven to 350°F. Line the bottom of a 9-inch springform pan with foil or parchment paper. Coat bottom and sides well with cooking spray.

2. **Prepare the crust:** In a large bowl, whisk together melted margarine and brown sugar. Add almonds, cocoa, and vanilla. Fold in oats. Transfer mixture to prepared pan; smooth evenly but don't press down hard. Bake 15 minutes. Set aside to cool.

3. **Prepare the ice cream:** In the large bowl of an electric mixer fitted with the whisk, beat nondairy whipping cream until stiff peaks form. Add eggs, one at a time, mixing until combined. Add corn syrup and vanilla. Stir to combine. Pour ice cream batter over cooled crust. Smooth with a spatula. Freeze for at least 1 hour until ice cream layer is frozen solid.

4. **Prepare the chocolate fudge layer:** In a 1-quart saucepan, combine chocolate pudding, water, and oil. Whisk constantly over medium heat until smooth and thickened. Remove from heat; stir in corn syrup. Refrigerate to cool.

5. Pour cooled fudge over frozen ice cream layer; freeze until solid.

6. **To serve:** Release springform, slice, and enjoy!

—Tip—

To achieve beautiful slices, as pictured, fill a cup with hot water and dip the knife into it before each cut. You can use this tip with any frozen dessert.

CARAMEL APPLE CRUMBLE

Pareve **YIELDS** *8-10 servings*

Crisp apples, creamy caramel sauce, and a fantastic crumb topping combine to make this completely irresistible.

Caramel Apples

5	firm apples (Granny Smith, Pink Lady, or Gala)
⅓ cup	sugar
⅓ cup	dark brown sugar
3 Tbsp	flour
¼ tsp	ground cardamom
½ tsp	ground cinnamon
1 tsp	sea salt
2 Tbsp	lemon juice
1 tsp	pure vanilla extract
1 tsp	almond extract
1 Tbsp	margarine, finely diced

Caramel Crumbs

½ cup	margarine (1 stick), diced
½ cup	dark brown sugar
1 cup	flour
¼ tsp	cinnamon
⅛ tsp	ground cardamom

Caramel Sauce

1 cup	sugar
⅓ cup	light corn syrup
2½ Tbsp	water
4 Tbsp	margarine, cubed and softened
½ tsp	pure vanilla extract
½ cup	nondairy whipping cream, at room temperature
•	nondairy vanilla ice cream, for serving

1. Preheat oven to 400°F. Set out 2 (9x13-inch) baking pans.

2. Peel and core apples. Quarter each apple. Cut each quarter into 3, yielding 12 wedges per apple.

3. Combine remaining caramel apple ingredients in one 9x13-inch pan. Add apple wedges. Toss to completely coat wedges. Bake, uncovered, on center rack for 15 minutes. Toss apples; bake for an additional 10 minutes. Remove apples from oven. Set aside to cool.

4. **Prepare the caramel crumbs:** Combine caramel crumb ingredients in the second 9x13-inch pan. Bake, uncovered, for 10 minutes. (Margarine should have melted.) Stir mixture until coarse crumbs form. Continue to bake for an additional 10 minutes, stirring every so often to break up clumps.

5. **Prepare the caramel sauce:** In a large skillet, over medium-high heat, cook sugar, corn syrup, and water without stirring, until honey colored (8-10 minutes). Remove from heat.

6. Add margarine, stirring until melted. Add vanilla. Gradually stir in nondairy whipping cream and kosher salt. Pour mixture into a bowl; allow to cool for 30 minutes.

7. **To serve:** Place several caramel apple wedges into a cup or bowl, or on the center of a plate. Place a scoop of ice cream over apples. Sprinkle with a handful of crumbs. Drizzle homemade or store-bought caramel sauce over apples. Apples can be served warm or at room temperature.

Note

Short on time? Store-bought caramel drizzle is a quick substitute topping.

CHOCOLATE CHIP COOKIE DOUGH ICE CREAM PIE

Pareve **YIELDS** *8 servings*

No-Bake Chocolate Chip Cookie Dough

8 Tbsp	flour
1 Tbsp	canola oil
2 Tbsp	light brown sugar, packed
2 Tbsp	powdered sugar
2 Tbsp	hazelnut praline cream (see Note)
1 Tbsp	nondairy milk
¼ tsp	pure vanilla extract
¼ tsp	sea salt
¼ cup	extra-mini chocolate chips
1 quart	nondairy vanilla ice cream, softened
¼ cup	Lotus Cookie Butter
1	prepared chocolate graham cracker crust
2 oz	good quality chocolate, melted, *or* store-bought chocolate and/or caramel drizzle

Satisfy your craving for chocolate chip cookie dough in a few short minutes with this no-bake, safe to eat, cookie dough-filled pie. Every bite of this Lotus-laden ice cream pie is sheer bliss. I always freeze an extra batch as this cookie dough freezes really well and is great for a quick snack, dessert, or just because.

1. **Prepare the chocolate chip cookie dough:** Measure flour into a small bowl. Microwave for 30 seconds to destroy any bacteria. Set aside. Prepare a baking sheet.

2. In a small bowl, stir together oil, sugars, and hazelnut praline cream until combined. Add nondairy milk and vanilla, stirring to incorporate. Add salt and flour; mix well. Stir in chocolate chips.

3. Roll half-teaspoons of cookie dough into small balls; place on prepared baking sheet. Repeat until all the dough is used. Place baking sheet into the freezer; freeze until solid. (Dough balls can be prepared in advance and frozen until ready to proceed.)

4. Place softened ice cream into a large bowl. Heat Lotus butter in the microwave for 15-20 seconds to liquify. Fold the warm Lotus butter into the softened ice cream, then stir in the frozen cookie dough balls. (If desired, reserve a few balls to decorate the top.) Pour ice cream into the graham cracker crust. Freeze until firm.

5. Drizzle pie with melted chocolate or chocolate and caramel drizzle. Top with reserved cookie dough balls, if using. Return pie to the freezer until ready to serve.

Variation

Switch up the flavor by substituting hazelnut praline cream with peanut butter, Lotus Cookie Butter, or almond butter.

Baked Goods

CARAMEL-GLAZED VANILLA BUNDT CAKE

Pareve   **YIELDS** *12 servings*

Every slice of this spectacular cake drizzled with caramel is a bit of pure goodness.

Vanilla Bundt Cake

1½ cups	canola oil
2 cups	sugar
1 cup	dark brown sugar, packed
5	eggs, at room temperature
1 Tbsp	pure vanilla extract
3 cups	flour
1 tsp	baking powder
½ tsp	kosher salt
1 cup	nondairy milk, at room temperature

Caramel Glaze

¼ cup	margarine
½ cup	dark brown sugar, packed
3 Tbsp	nondairy milk
1 cup	powdered sugar
1 tsp	pure vanilla extract

1. Preheat oven to 350°F. Grease and flour a 12-cup Bundt pan.

2. In the bowl of an electric mixer, beat oil and sugars at medium speed until combined. Scrape sides of bowl as needed. Add eggs, one at a time, beating well between each addition. Add vanilla, beating until combined.

3. In a medium bowl or large measuring cup, combine flour, baking powder, and salt.

4. With mixer on low speed, add one-third of flour mixture; beat until combined. Add ½ cup nondairy milk. Beat well between each addition until combined. Add another third of flour mixture. Add remaining ½ cup nondairy milk. Add remaining third of flour mixture. Mix until just combined.

5. Transfer batter to prepared Bundt pan. Bake on center rack for 1 hour 5 minutes. Cool for 10 minutes. Invert cake onto a cooling rack; cool completely.

6. **Prepare the caramel glaze:** In a small pot, over medium heat, melt together margarine, brown sugar, and nondairy milk, whisking constantly, until the mixture reaches a boil. Remove from heat; allow to cool for 10 minutes.

7. Add powdered sugar and vanilla; whisk until smooth. Pour or spoon glaze over cooled cake.

BEST-EVER BROWNIES

Pareve

YIELDS *1 (8-inch) square pan*

7 oz	good quality pareve chocolate, such as Noblesse
½ cup	canola oil
3 Tbsp	cocoa powder
3	eggs
1¼ cups	sugar
2 tsp	pure vanilla extract
½ tsp	sea salt
1 cup	flour

For years, I couldn't find a recipe for brownies that left me craving another piece. I was constantly testing ratios and combinations. Finally, I can say that this is the BEST brownie recipe! The rich, fudgy flavor is achieved by combining cocoa and melted chocolate. These brownies are now on repeat in my kitchen. My brownie quest is complete.

1. Preheat oven to 350°F. Grease and flour an 8-inch square pan.

2. In a double boiler, melt together chocolate, oil, and cocoa powder. Alternatively, microwave for 20-second intervals, stirring between intervals. Set aside.

3. In a medium bowl, whisk together eggs, sugar, vanilla, and salt until slightly thickened. Slowly add warm melted chocolate mixture, followed by flour. Continue to whisk until thoroughly combined. Transfer batter to prepared pan.

4. Bake 25-28 minutes, until slightly puffed. Cut into squares or bars. Brownies will harden as they cool.

NEW YORK-STYLE DOUBLE CRUMB LOAF

They say that you can't judge a book by its cover. Well, I say you CAN judge a crumb cake by its crumbs. I figured, why not double the crumbs and double the experience. With its signature sweet cinnamon streusel and equally delicious cake, you will enjoy each and every piece down to the last crumb.

Pareve   **YIELDS** *12 servings*

1 cup	sugar
½ cup	canola oil
2	eggs
1 Tbsp	vanilla sugar
2 cups	flour
¼ tsp	baking soda
1 tsp	baking powder
½ tsp	sea salt
1 Tbsp	lemon juice
¾ cup	nondairy milk, less 1 Tbsp

New York-Style Crumbs

⅔ cup	flour
⅓ cup	powdered sugar
⅓ cup	light brown sugar, packed
½ Tbsp	vanilla sugar
5 Tbsp	canola oil
½ tsp	cinnamon

1. Preheat oven to 350°F. Grease a 9½-inch loaf pan.

2. **Prepare the New York-style crumbs:** In a small mixing bowl, combine crumb ingredients. Mix until crumbs form. Set aside.

3. **Prepare the batter:** In a large mixing bowl, whisk together sugar, oil, eggs, and vanilla sugar, until lemon-colored and thickened. In a second bowl, combine flour, baking soda, baking powder, and salt. Add lemon juice to a measuring cup. Add nondairy milk until it reaches ¾ cup.

4. Alternate adding flour mixture and nondairy milk mixture into the egg mixture. Whisk until a smooth batter forms. Transfer batter to prepared loaf pan.

5. Sprinkle crumbs over cake, beginning at the outer edge of the pan toward the center. Cover the entire top well with crumbs.

6. Place pan into oven. Rest a piece of parchment paper on the pan. This will prevent the crumbs from browning too quickly.

7. Bake for 60-70 minutes. Test for doneness with toothpick; toothpick should come out clean.

—Tip

This recipe can be easily doubled to yield 2 loaves, 1 Bundt cake, or a 9x13-inch cake.

—Note

This loaf cake is doubly delicious topped with whipped cream, mint leaves, and fresh fruit, as pictured.

BABKA BUNDT CAKE

Pareve **YIELDS** *12 servings*

When I first made this cake, one of my children sliced into it and exclaimed, "Ma! This looks like babka!" The batter is so rich and filled with chocolatey goodness, there wasn't a crumb left. I was almost tempted to call it "The Disappearing Bundt Cake."

Cake

2¾ cups	flour
1½ tsp	baking powder
1½ tsp	baking soda
½ tsp	sea salt
¾ cup	canola oil
1½ cups	sugar
1 Tbsp	pure vanilla extract
3	eggs
1 Tbsp	lemon juice
1½ cups	nondairy milk, less 1 Tbsp

Babka Filling

¾ cup	dark brown sugar, packed
2 Tbsp	cocoa powder
1 Tbsp	cinnamon
•	powdered sugar, for dusting

1. In a small bowl, combine babka filling ingredients. Mix well; set aside.

2. Preheat oven to 350°F. Grease and flour a 10-12-cup Bundt pan; set aside.

3. In a medium bowl, combine flour, baking powder, baking soda, and salt. Set aside.

4. In the large bowl of an electric mixer, beat together oil, sugar, and vanilla. Add eggs, one at a time, beating well after each addition. Scrape the sides of the bowl with a spatula as needed.

5. Add 1 tablespoon lemon juice to a 2-cup measure. Add nondairy milk until the 1½-cup mark. Mix well; let stand.

6. Add half the flour mixture to the mixer bowl. Beat on low speed until combined. Add half the nondairy milk; beat until combined. Scrape sides as necessary. Repeat with remaining flour mixture and nondairy milk. Beat just until mixture is smooth.

7. Pour one-third of the batter into prepared Bundt pan. Spread half the babka filling over batter. Cover filling with another third of the batter; top with remaining babka filling. Top with remaining batter, for a total of 3 layers of batter and 2 layers of filling.

8. Bake on the center rack for 1 hour, until a toothpick comes out dry. Remove cake from oven. After 5 minutes, loosen sides; turn out onto a cooling rack. Once cool, dust with powdered sugar.

MAPLE PECAN CRUMB MUFFINS

Pareve

YIELDS *2 dozen muffins*

3	eggs
¾ cup	oil
¾ cup	nondairy milk
¾ cup	sugar
¾ cup	pure maple syrup
1 Tbsp	baking powder
1 tsp	pure vanilla extract
½ tsp	sea salt
3 cups	flour

Maple Pecan Crumbs

1 cup	flour
¾ cup	chopped pecans, preferably toasted
¼ cup	dark brown sugar
6 Tbsp	canola oil
6 Tbsp	pure maple syrup
1 tsp	cinnamon

Bourbon Glaze, optional

1½ cups	powdered sugar
1 Tbsp	pure maple syrup
1 Tbsp	bourbon
1 Tbsp	canola oil
1 tsp	pure vanilla extract
2-3 tsp	boiling water

While I was knee deep in recipe development, writing, and testing, my talented friend, Miriam (Pascal) Cohen, called to see how it was going. Understanding the pressure, she made me an offer I couldn't refuse. Thank you, Miriam, for these fantastic muffins with their subtle touch of maple and pecan crunch.

1. Preheat oven to 350°F. Line muffin pans with paper liners; set aside.

2. **Prepare the maple pecan crumbs:** In a small bowl, combine all crumb ingredients. Mix to combine. The mixture will be wet and sticky. Set aside.

3. **Prepare the batter:** In a large bowl, whisk together eggs, oil, nondairy milk, sugar, maple syrup, baking powder, vanilla, and salt. Add flour; mix until just combined.

4. Spoon batter into prepared muffin pans, filling each cup about three-quarters full. Top each with a generous layer of maple pecan crumbs.

5. Bake for 18-20 minutes, until the tops are set. Remove from oven; allow to cool.

6. **Prepare the optional bourbon glaze:** In a small bowl, combine all bourbon glaze ingredients. Drizzle over completely cooled muffins.

RASPBERRY RIBBONS

Pareve

YIELDS *about 6 dozen ribbons*

1 cup	margarine (2 sticks), softened
½ cup	sugar
1	egg
2 Tbsp	nondairy milk
2 Tbsp	pure vanilla extract
¼ tsp	almond extract
2⅔ cups	flour
6 heaping Tbsp	seedless raspberry jam

Glaze

½ cup	powdered sugar
1 Tbsp	nondairy milk
1 tsp	pure vanilla extract

Thank you, Chani G., for sharing these insanely delicious ribbons with me! They always disappear in the blink of an eye and are truly on another level.

1. In the large bowl of an electric mixer fitted with the cookie paddle(s), beat margarine and sugar at medium speed. Add egg, nondairy milk, vanilla, and almond extract. Beat until blended. Add flour. Beat on low speed until well blended and a stiff dough forms. Wrap dough in plastic wrap; refrigerate until firm (at least 30 minutes).

2. Preheat oven to 375°F. Line a baking sheet with parchment paper.

3. Divide dough into 6 pieces. With floured hands, shape each piece into a 12-inch-long (¾-inch-thick) log. Place logs 2 inches apart on prepared baking sheet. Make a ¼-inch deep groove down the center of each log by pressing down lengthwise with the handle of a wooden spoon.

4. Bake 12 minutes. Remove pan from oven. Reinforce the indentation on each log by again pressing down with the handle of wooden spoon. Spoon 1 tablespoon jam along each groove. Bake an additional 5-7 minutes until golden brown. Cool for 15 minutes.

5. **Prepare the glaze:** In a medium bowl, whisk together glaze ingredients until smooth. Drizzle glaze over logs.

6. Cut each log into 1-inch slices at a 45° angle. Store ribbons in an airtight container at room temperature with parchment paper between layers.

CINNAMON CITRUS BISCOTTI

Pareve **YIELDS** *24 biscotti*

I was hesitant to develop another biscotti recipe, uncertain that I could come up with one to rival my go-to Chocolate Chip Biscotti on my Instagram page. I am glad I challenged myself, because the subtle cinnamon and citrus flavors make these the perfect accompaniment to your morning coffee or tea.

1 cup	sugar
½ cup	canola oil
2	eggs
•	zest of 1 orange (2 tsp)
1 tsp	pure vanilla extract
1 tsp	orange extract
2¼ cups	flour
1½ tsp	baking powder
1 tsp	cinnamon
¼ tsp	sea salt

Citrus Glaze

1 cup	powdered sugar
2 Tbsp	canola oil
¾ Tbsp	orange zest
2-3 Tbsp	orange juice (for desired consistency)

1. Preheat oven to 325°F. Line a baking sheet with parchment paper.

2. In the large bowl of an electric mixer fitted with the paddle(s) attachment, beat sugar and oil until blended. Add eggs, one at a time, beating well after each addition. Add zest and extracts, beating until combined. Gradually add flour, baking powder, cinnamon, and salt. Mix until incorporated.

3. Divide dough into 2 or 3 parts on the prepared baking sheet. With moistened hands, form into logs. (Dividing dough in 2 will yield 2 long logs. Dividing dough in 3 will yield 3 short logs.)

4. Bake for 35-40 minutes. Remove from oven; cool for 10 minutes. Slice into 1-inch slices. If you enjoy crispier biscotti, turn each slice on its side; return to oven and bake 2-3 minutes longer. Repeat on the second side. Let biscotti cool completely.

5. **Prepare the glaze:** In a small bowl, whisk together glaze ingredients. Drizzle glaze over cooled biscotti.

SNICKERDOODLE STIX

Pareve **YIELDS** *36 sticks*

1 cup sugar

⅔ cup light brown sugar

2 eggs

1 cup canola oil

1 tsp pure vanilla extract

3 cups flour

¾ tsp kosher salt

1 tsp baking soda

½ tsp cream of tartar (see Note)

Topping

¼ cup sugar

2 tsp cinnamon

As a little girl, I was obsessed with snickerdoodle cookies. My mother used to bake a batch and send some with me to school for snack. Boy, was I popular! I decided to give the recipe an update. When I enjoy these stix, I am filled with delicious childhood memories.

1. In the bowl of an electric mixture fitted with the cookie paddle(s), beat together sugars and eggs on high speed. Slowly add oil and vanilla, mixing until combined.

2. Gradually add flour, salt, baking soda, and cream of tartar, beating until well mixed and a soft dough forms. Refrigerate dough for 1 hour.

3. Preheat oven to 350°F. Line a baking sheet with parchment paper.

4. **Prepare the topping:** In a small bowl, combine topping ingredients. Mix well. Sprinkle 3 sections of prepared baking sheet with ½ tablespoon topping each.

5. Divide dough into 3 parts. Shape each piece into a flat 3x10-inch bar over the sprinkled topping. Sprinkle remaining topping over the bars.

6. Bake on center rack of oven for 25-30 minutes. Remove from oven. Cool for 5 minutes; slice into sticks.

— Note

If you don't have cream of tartar, you can substitute with baking powder, but it will yield a chewier texture.

RED VELVET CHOCOLATE CHIP COOKIES

Pareve

YIELDS *30 large cookies or 40 small cookies*

½ **cup**	canola oil
¾ **cup**	dark brown sugar, packed
¼ **cup**	sugar
1	egg
1 Tbsp	red food coloring
2 tsp	pure vanilla extract
1½ **cups**	flour
¼ **cup**	cocoa
1 tsp	baking soda
¼ **tsp**	sea salt
1 cup	semisweet chocolate chips + more for post baking, optional

I am a tried and true red velvet cake fan. These cookies are the perfect combination in which classic red velvet cake meets chewy, crunchy chocolate chip cookie. What more could you ask for?!

1. Preheat oven to 350°F. Line 2 baking sheets with parchment paper.

2. In the large bowl of an electric mixer fitted with the cookie paddle(s), beat oil and sugars, scraping down the sides, until combined. Beat in egg, food coloring, and vanilla extract, scraping down the bottom and sides as needed.

3. Turn off the mixer. Add flour, cocoa, baking soda, and salt. Turn the mixer on low; slowly beat until a soft dough forms. Add chocolate chips; beat until combined. You may refrigerate the dough or scoop it into balls and then refrigerate.

4. Roll 1 tablespoon dough into a ball. (I use an ice cream scoop.) Place on prepared baking sheet. Repeat with remaining dough.

5. Bake cookies for 8-10 minutes. Allow cookies to cool for 5 minutes; transfer to a cooling rack. If desired, you can press additional chocolate chips into the warm cookies.

CINNABUN COOKIES

Dairy

YIELDS *about 24 cookies*

¾ cup	butter (1½ sticks), softened to room temperature
½ cup	powdered sugar
1½ tsp	pure vanilla extract
½ tsp	sea salt
1½ cups	flour
3 Tbsp	butter, melted

Cinnamon Filling

⅓ cup	light brown sugar, packed
2½ tsp	cinnamon
⅛ tsp	sea salt

With their melt-in-your-mouth buttery goodness, these cookies are the perfect choice for any dairy occasion. I have used these to decorate my cinnabun cheesecake as well as to fill my family cookie jar.

1. In the large bowl of an electric mixer fitted with the cookie paddle(s), cream butter, sugar, vanilla, and salt. Add flour. Mix until dough comes together. Flatten dough into a disc, wrap in plastic wrap, close tightly, and refrigerate for 1 hour until the dough is firm (not hardened). If refrigerated overnight, allow dough to soften until easy to handle.

2. Transfer chilled dough to a lightly floured piece of parchment paper. Top dough with a second piece of parchment paper. Roll dough into a 9x12-inch rectangle. Remove the top piece of parchment paper. Brush melted butter over the dough.

3. **Prepare the cinnamon filling:** In a small bowl, combine filling ingredients. Spread mixture evenly over dough.

4. Starting with the long edge, carefully roll the dough into a log (deli-roll style), making sure to seal tightly. Wrap log in the parchment paper; freeze until firm.

5. Preheat oven to 350°F. Line 2 baking sheets with parchment paper.

6. Remove log from the freezer. Unwrap; gently cut into ½-inch slices with a very sharp knife. Place cookies on prepared baking sheet. Bake for 12 minutes, until lightly browned.

—Tip
It is very important that the butter is softened at room temperature or the dough will be crumbly.

—Variation
Substitute margarine for the butter for pareve cookies.

OREO CHEESECAKE-FILLED FUDGY CHOCOLATE THUMBPRINTS

Dairy **YIELDS** *4 dozen cookies*

Calling all cheesecake and Oreo lovers! This fudgy, buttery cookie is chock-full of yummy crushed Oreos, beyond delicious, and super easy to make. In one word, they are simply WOW!

Fudgy Thumbprints

2 oz	Noblesse or other good quality chocolate
½ cup	butter (1 stick)
1 cup	light brown sugar
½ tsp	pure vanilla extract
1	egg
2 cups	flour
½ tsp	baking powder
¼ tsp	sea salt

No-Bake Oreo Cheesecake Filling

2 oz	good quality white chocolate or two-toned Harmony chocolate, chopped finely
½ cup + 2 Tbsp	heavy cream, divided
12 oz	cream cheese (1½ bars)
¾ cup	powdered sugar
¼ cup	crushed Oreo cookie crumbs

1. **Prepare the fudgy thumbprints:** Break chocolate into small pieces. Microwave at 20-second intervals, stirring each time, until melted. Set aside.

2. In the large bowl of an electric mixer fitted with the cookie paddle(s), beat butter, sugar, and vanilla until smooth. Add melted chocolate; beat until combined. Add egg, beating until incorporated. Gradually add flour, baking powder, and salt until well blended. Transfer dough to plastic wrap. Form into a log or disc. Seal well; refrigerate for 30 minutes.

3. Preheat oven to 350°F. Line a baking sheet with parchment paper.

4. Shape dough into 1-inch balls (a small scoop works well here). Place balls onto prepared baking sheet. Make an indentation in the center of each ball with your thumb. Bake for 7-8 minutes. Remove from oven to cool. If necessary, press down on indentation while cooling.

5. **Prepare the cheesecake filling:** In a medium bowl, combine chopped chocolate with 2 tablespoons heavy cream. Microwave at 20-second intervals, stirring each time, until mixture is smooth and completely melted. Set aside.

6. In the large bowl of an electric mixer, beat cream cheese until smooth. Add powdered sugar, beating until combined. While beating, slowly add melted chocolate mixture. Add remaining ½ cup heavy cream; beat until peaks form. Beat in cookie crumbs.

7. Once thumbprints are cool, pipe or spoon cheesecake filling into the center of each thumbprint.

8. Refrigerate cookies. Enjoy chilled or at room temperature.

Simple Supper

SIMPLE S SUPPER

The day begins with the **shrill of the alarm clock ringing**.
As you **wipe the sleep** from your eyes,
your brain is already **kicking into high gear**.

The endless **daily to-do list** looms, **insurmountable**.

Divide and conquer ... **Breathe in, breathe out ...**
Always trying to stay a step ahead.

Every day, **evening creeps** in with a **mild panic** and a **major question**:

"What's for supper?"

Allow me to put it

SIMPLY.

Turn the pages and you will see, just how easy supper can be.

Follow the tips, learn the tricks. You too can achieve

SIMPLY GOURMET, EVERY DAY

SIMPLE SUPPER

In addition to the recipes featured on these pages, here are more Simple Suppers that can be found throughout the book.

BBQ BEEF WITH ORECCHIETTE

page 182

Pairs with:

QUICK BROCCOLI BISQUE, page 106

HOUSE SALAD, PAREVE VERSION, page 84

PREP 15 MIN
COOK 20 MIN

35 MIN

FROM START TO FINISH

TIPS AND TRICKS

Buy a family pack of ground beef and prepare a double batch.

Double the sauce; freeze half for the next time.

ADDITIONAL USES FOR BBQ BEEF MIXTURE

Add to tacos with veggies and condiments of choice.

Serve as Sloppy Joes.

Stuff into egg roll wrappers for a great appetizer.

PREP AHEAD

Both the BBQ beef mixture and the orecchiette can be prepared and refrigerated separately the night before or early in the day. Reheat beef mixture; mix with pasta before serving.

Simple Suppers

SIMPLE S SUPPER

PREP **3 MIN**
COOK **10 MIN**

13 MIN

FROM START TO FINISH

CHILI-LIME HANGER STEAK
page 192

HERB MARINATED LONDON BROIL
page 194

Pairs well with:

SOY-GLAZED EDAMAME, page 234

GLAZED ZUCCHINI SPEARS, page 222

PREP **15 MIN**
COOK **8 MIN**

24 MIN

FROM START TO FINISH

PREP AHEAD

Marinade can be prepared the night before.
Meat should only be added up to 8 hours before
grilling since prolonged marinating in the acidic
mixture can make the meat mushy.

TIPS AND TRICKS

Substitute for the skirt steak in Grilled Skirt Steak Salad
(page 96) or top your favorite salad to make it a full meal.

Prepare a few at a time and freeze: Add to marinade in a
resealable bag; freeze immediately. Defrost when ready to use.

Although it can be pricey for a large family,
this is a great supper for two or for a few guests.

306

GARLICKY MEATBALLS

page 178

Pairs with:

SPAGHETTI, MASHED POTATOES, OR RICE

HONEY-MUSTARD KALE SALAD, page 86

SILKY ASPARAGUS SOUP, page 110

PREP 5 MIN
COOK 40 MIN

45 MIN

FROM START TO FINISH

TIPS AND TRICKS

Buy a family pack of ground beef and prepare a double batch. Meatballs freeze beautifully. I find it better to freeze prepared meatballs than to freeze raw ground beef as is.

Prepare the meatball mixture, form meatballs, and place on a baking sheet. Freeze solid; then transfer to a resealable bag. Once ready for use, semi-defrost and bake or cook in sauce.

PREP AHEAD

Raw meatball mixture can be prepared the night before and refrigerated until ready for use.

Meatballs can be cooked the night before or early in the day. Reheat over low heat before serving, stirring occasionally.

Simple Suppers

SIMPLE S SUPPER

CRISPY BAKED
LEMON-HERB CHICKEN

page 164

Pairs with:

RAIZEL'S FAVORITE QUINOA SALAD (PICTURED), page 78

JAPANESE YAM SPEARS, page 236

SOY-GLAZED EDAMAME, page 234

PREP 7 MIN
COOK 30 MIN

37 MIN

FROM START TO FINISH

TIPS AND TRICKS

Buy a family pack of cutlets. Line a 9x13-inch pan with parchment paper. Bread the cutlets and place a layer into the pan. Top with another piece of parchment paper; continue to layer breaded cutlets. You can prepare multiple layers in one pan, which saves freezer space.

Remove the number of breaded cutlets that you need; return the remainder to the freezer.

Completely defrost cutlets in a single layer before baking/frying.

THESE TRICKS WILL WORK ON ANY BREADED CUTLETS

PREP AHEAD

Prepare a large batch of crumbs in advance.
Divide between resealable bags. Label and freeze.

BEST-DRESSED CHICKEN CUTLETS
page 166

PERFECT PARGIYOT WITH CHIMICHURRI SAUCE
page 168

These marinated chicken cutlets pair with:

SUGAR SNAP PEA STIR FRY (PICTURED),
page 230

LETTUCE SALAD WITH
YOUR FAVORITE DRESSING,
page 100-101

SAVORY SWEET POTATO SOUP,
page 104

POTATOES OR RICE SIDE
OF CHOICE

PREP **3 MIN**
COOK **6-10 MIN**

13 MIN

FROM START TO FINISH

PREP **3 MIN**
COOK **15 MIN**

18 MIN

FROM START TO FINISH

TIPS AND TRICKS

Prepare a double batch (or more) of the
marinade; divide between resealable bags.

Add chicken to the marinade, toss to
completely coat. Press chicken into a single
layer in the marinade.

Immediately place your extra batch(es) into
the freezer, preferably lying flat.

Defrost when ready for use.

PREP AHEAD

Clean chicken and prepare marinade separately
the night before or early in the day; refrigerate.

Chimichurri can be made in advance and stored
in the refrigerator.

Simple Suppers

SIMPLE **S** SUPPER

CHICKEN WITH PESTO, SHALLOT, AND WHITE WINE SAUCE

page 172

Pairs with:

CREAMY DILL SLAW (PICTURED), page 72

VELVETY MUSHROOM LEEK SOUP, page 112

SPINACH MUSHROOM RICE, page 214

**PREP 12 MIN
COOK 3 MIN
15 MIN**
FROM START TO FINISH

TIPS AND TRICKS

As with any breaded chicken, after marinating the chicken, dredge in the cornstarch; refrigerate, uncovered, for an hour to overnight. This will yield an epic crisp to the chicken.

To ensure even cooking, remove chicken from fridge at least 15 minutes before frying.

PREP AHEAD

Prepare the chicken the night before or early in the day.

Prepare the Pesto, Shallot, and White Wine Sauce the night before.

PREP 10 MIN
COOK 1 HR 30 MIN
1 HR 40 MIN
FROM START TO FINISH

CRANBBQ CHICKEN BAKE
page 148

HONEY-MUSTARD DRUMSTICKS
page 150

Although technically not a simple supper based on the time it takes to get dinner on the table, I decided to dedicate a page to bone-in chicken, as it truly is so short on prep time that it does fit into the category.

Pairs with:

SALT-BAKED GARLIC-ROASTED POTATOES, page 238
CARAMELIZED MUSHROOMS (PICTURED), page 228
CHUNKY ROOT VEGETABLE SOUP, page 114
HONEY-LIME NUT SALAD, page 92

PREP 10 MIN
COOK 1 HR 30 MIN
1 HR 35 MIN
FROM START TO FINISH

TIPS AND TRICKS

Prepare multiple pans with the number of pieces of cleaned chicken you will need to prepare a dinner.

Add spices, or spice and dress with your favorite glazes, as you can prepare a variety of glazes; just be sure to label before you freeze. Defrost when ready to use.

PREP AHEAD

For the CranBBQ Chicken: Prepare potatoes and chicken the night before or early in the day. Add spices; refrigerate until ready to bake.
Prepare cranBBQ or honey-mustard glaze; refrigerate.

Cook larges batches of soups. Once cooled, divide between multiple containers.
Label and freeze. Defrost soup of choice; reheat slowly, stirring occasionally.

Simple Suppers

SIMPLE S SUPPER

SPINACH FLOUNDER ROLL-UPS

Page 128

Pairs with:

PENNE WITH ROASTED VEGGETABLES
(PICTURED), page 50

STICKY SMASHED POTATOES, page 242

PREP **10 MIN**
COOK **20 MIN**

30 MIN

FROM START TO FINISH

TIPS AND TRICKS

Freeze roll-ups uncovered until frozen
solid, then cover with plastic wrap or foil to
avoid smearing the topping.

PREP AHEAD

Prepare the Spinach Flounder Roll-Ups
earlier in the day. Bake when ready to serve.

You can completely prepare this dish and freeze it
raw. Defrost and bake when ready to serve.

SIMPLE S SUPPER

CAULIFLOWER CRUSTED SALMON

page 140

Pairs with:

JAPANESE YAM SPEARS
(PICTURED) page 236

STICKY GREEN BEANS
page 226

HONEY-MUSTARD KALE SALAD
page 86

WHITE BEAN SOUP
page 108

PREP **25 MIN**
COOK **17 MIN**

FROM START TO FINISH

42 MIN

PREP AHEAD

Make cauliflower crust the night before;
refrigerate until ready to use.

Prepare the dip in advance as well, or, if short
on time, use a store-bought dip.

TIPS AND TRICKS

For the perfect bake, remove fish from the fridge
15 minutes before cooking to bring it to an even
temperature prior to preparing it.

Simple Suppers

SIMPLE S SUPPER

SIMPLY SAVORY
SALMON

page 142

Pairs with:

CRUNCHY CAULIFLOWER
POPPERS (PICTURED), page 18

THE UPPER CRUST
SWEET POTATO SALAD, page 82

EASY CHEESY
CAULIFLOWER SOUP, page 118

RICE SIDE OF CHOICE

PREP 3 MIN
COOK 17 MIN

20 MIN

FROM START TO FINISH

TIPS AND TRICKS

Always pat seafood dry with a paper
towel. This will ensure an even bake
and prevent the top of the fish from
getting tough or mushy.

SIMPLE S

Fish generally need very little cooking time and meals come together quickly. Here are a few fabulous pairings that might inspire you to make a simple supper in record time.

EVERYTHING BAGEL SPICED TURBOT

page 132

Pairs with:

HERBED CAULIFLOWER RICE, page 224

PREP 1 MIN
COOK 7 MIN

8 MIN
FROM START TO FINISH

PREP 5 MIN
COOK 15 MIN

20 MIN
FROM START TO FINISH

GARLICKY CITRUS BRANZINO

page 136

Pairs with:

BLACKENED BROCCOLI, page 232

TO COMPLETE THESE DINNERS, CONSIDER ADDING

FRESH SPINACH FETTUCCINE, page 48

RAVIOLI WITH MUSHROOM VODKA SAUCE, page 52

(This dish requires more than 15 minutes.)

PREP 4 MIN
COOK 2 MIN

6 MIN
FROM START TO FINISH

SEARED TUNA WITH WHITE WINE VINAIGRETTE

page 134

Pairs with:

STICKY GREEN BEANS, page 226

315

INDEX

Index